The Scapegoat Complex

Marie-Louise von Franz, Honorary Patron

**Studies in Jungian Psychology
by Jungian Analysts**

Daryl Sharp, General Editor

The Scapegoat Complex

Toward a Mythology of
Shadow and Guilt

Sylvia Brinton Perera

Some of the material presented here first appeared in *Quadrant* (Journal
of the C.G. Jung Foundation for Analytical Psychology, New York), volume
12, number 2 (Winter 1979).

Canadian Cataloguing in Publication Data

Perera, Sylvia Brinton, 1932-
    The scapegoat complex

(Studies in Jungian psychology by Jungian analysts; 23)

Bibliography: p.
Includes index.

ISBN 0-919123-22-8

1. Guilt—Psychological aspects. 2. Scapegoat—
Psychological aspects. 3. Jung, C.G. (Carl Gustav),
1875-1961. I. Title. II. Series.

BF575.G8P47 1986   155.2   C86-093399-7

INNER CITY BOOKS
Box 1271, Station Q, Toronto, Canada M4T 2P4
Telephone (416) 927-0355

INNER CITY BOOKS was founded in 1980 to promote the
understanding and practical application of the work of C.G. Jung.

Cover: Detail of *God Judging Adam,* water color by William Blake,
1795. (The Tate Gallery, London)

Index by Daryl Sharp

Printed and bound in Canada by Webcom Limited

CONTENTS

See final pages for descriptions of other Inner City Books

If only it were all so simple! If only there were evil people somewhere insidiously committing evil deeds, and it were necessary only to separate them from the rest of us and destroy them. But the line dividing good and evil cuts through the heart of every human being. And who is willing to destroy a piece of his own heart?

—Alexander Solzhenitsyn, *The Gulag Archipelago.*

Preface

The material in this book owes much to others. Many friends have given me their personal support. Among these are Jerome Bernstein, Edward Edinger, Patricia Finley, Yoram Kaufmann, Katherine North, Barbara Sand, Nathan Schwartz-Salant, Charles Taylor and Gertrude Ujhely. While the insights into the material are of my own crafting, I have been helped by their stimulating points of view.

I am particularly indebted to E. Christopher Whitmont for the many dialogues in which we explored the scapegoat myth and its ramifications. I have been most interested in its clinical relevance. His own important material in *Return of the Goddess* deals with broader cultural implications of the scapegoat image, as does Eric Neumann's *Depth Psychology and a New Ethic*.

The works of D.W. Winnicott and Harry Guntrip provide cogent clinical descriptions that initially sparked my interest in the psychology of the schizoid personality and led me to think about it in terms of underlying mythic patterns.

I want also to state my gratitude to the late Anneliese Aumueller and to Edward Edinger and Rachel Zahn for helping me in my own therapy to work through embeddedness in the scapegoat complex.

Above all I am grateful to those colleagues, friends, students and analysands who have shared their experiences with me. Their material and my own have illuminated the difficult core around which this book grew.

While I do not deal here with the broader problems of shadow projection that lead to war and are the basis of collective scapegoating of "enemy" shadow carriers, I hope that my work derived from individual depth analysis will encourage others to deal with the societal implications of the scapegoat archetype. My descriptions of its effects and healing in therapy are only a step toward the necessary healing of collective scapegoat pathology that threatens the survival of our earth.

Introduction

Today we use the term "scapegoat" easily in discussions of collective morality. We have become attuned to finding the phenomenon of scapegoating in social psychology, and there are many studies of the scapegoat pattern in small groups, in families, in ethnic and national politics.

We apply the term to individuals and groups who are accused of causing misfortune. This serves to relieve others, the scapegoaters, of their own responsibilities, and to strengthen the scapegoaters' sense of power and righteousness. In this current usage a search for the scapegoat relieves us also of our relationship to the transpersonal dimension of life, for in the present age we have come to function with a perverted form of the archetype, one that ignores the gods, and we blame the scapegoat and the devil for life's evils.

We forget that originally the scapegoat was a human or animal victim chosen for sacrifice to the underworld god to propitiate that god's anger and to heal the community. The scapegoat was a *pharmakon* or healing agent. In the scapegoat rituals it was dedicated to and identified with the god. It functioned to bring the transpersonal dimension to aid and renew the community, for the community acknowledged that it was embedded in and dependent on transpersonal forces. The scapegoat ritual, like others, was used "to enrich meaning or call attention to other levels of existence. . . . [It] incorporate[d] evil and death along with life and goodness into a single, grand, unifying pattern."[1]

Today we still believe in the efficacy of magic ritual action. But we are too often unconscious of the "grand, unifying pattern," the transpersonal matrix in which our actions are embedded. We see only the material, secular framework of the actions and ignore the spiritual dimension to which they were originally intended to connect us. Thus a modern psychologist writes:

> [There is] a general Western belief that catastrophe can be averted by the appropriate prophylactic action, whether it be baptism or breast feeding. We would like to believe in a prescription . . . that can innoculate . . . against future misery and failure.[2]

This desire to avert catastrophe is worldwide and forms the basis

8

of religious and magic ritual. In the modern age, however, the scapegoat ritual has gone bad because it has become trivialized. Its deeper meaning is unconscious. We tend to feel that mankind and/or the devil bring evil into the world, since God is only good. But this means that mankind is also felt to be nearly omnipotent, capable of averting evil without recourse to those forces of destiny far greater than human will.

Scapegoating, as it is currently practiced, means finding the one or ones who can be identified with evil or wrong-doing, blamed for it, and cast out from the community in order to leave the remaining members with a feeling of guiltlessness, atoned (at-one) with the collective standards of behavior. It both allocates blame and serves to "innoculate against future misery and failure" by evicting the presumed cause of misfortune. It gives the illusion that we can be "perfect, even as your Father which is in heaven is perfect,"[3] if we take the proper prophylactic measures, do the right things.

In Jungian terms, scapegoating is a form of denying the shadow of both man and God. What is seen as unfit to conform with the ego ideal, or with the perfect goodness of God, is repressed and denied, or split off and made unconscious. It is called devilish. We do not consciously confess our faults and wayward impulses over the scapegoat's head in order to atone with the spiritual dimension as did the ancient Hebrews. We do not often enough even see that they are part of our psychological make-up. But we are acutely aware of their belonging to others, the scapegoats. We see the shadow clearly in projection. And the scapegoater feels a relief in being lighter, without the burden of carrying what is unacceptable to his or her ego ideal, without shadow. Those who are identified with the scapegoat, on the other hand, are identified with the unacceptable shadow qualities. They feel inferior, rejected and guilty. They feel responsible for more than their personal share of shadow. But both scapegoater and scapegoat feel in control of the mix of goodness and malevolence that belongs to reality itself.

The medieval and modern perversion of the archetype has produced a pathology that is widespread. There are many scapegoats among us, individuals identified with the archetype and caught in the distorted pattern in which it now operates. In the following pages I will explore some of the ramifications of the scapegoat archetype as it applies to the clinical phenomenology of scapegoat-identified individuals. The image of the scapegoat provides vectors of comprehension that illuminate what is behind a common dis-ease felt by many of us. Thus, in C.G. Jung's words, it permits "consciousness . . . [to be] born of unconsciousness."[4] Following the layers of the complex in its current pathological form down into the structures of the original archetypal image provides clues for the healing of individuals caught in the scapegoat complex.

Readers will need to proceed slowly and to remember that, although the material here is necessarily presented in linear form, its focus is on the total gestalt—the immediate and whole structure of the archetypal image. The many factors described exist simultaneously in the timeless and dense pattern of the image itself.

My understanding is derived from my own experience of the complex, from material shared by friends and from clinical work with analysands. The scapegoat complex is widespread. To some extent we all share its salient features, although these are most clearly seen in certain cases. The difference is one of degree of identification with the archetype and hence weakness of ego. The structure of the complex remains the same.

1

The Riddance of Evil and Guilt

The Hebrew scapegoat sacrifice described in the Bible (Leviticus 16) was a central part of the Yom Kippur ritual. Comparable atonement and riddance-of-evil ceremonies in many cultures have been described by James George Frazer and other anthropologists.[5] They all represent a means of renewing contact with the guiding spirit of the people. They also are an attempt to excise the evils that afflict mankind, whether these be death, disease, violence, physical and psychic sufferings, or the sense of sin and guilt that accompanies knowledge of transgression of the moral code. Always such afflictions threaten to press us into the darkness and disorder that we meet both outside and inside ourselves. Throughout history, mankind has tried to thrust that darkness away with rites of aversion and riddance, hoping to avoid its dreaded pains and guilt.

In ceremonies of riddance the evil is magically transferred to other persons, to animals, plants or inanimate objects. The evil is treated concretely, as if it were a contagion that could be drawn off into a material object which then becomes—on the concrete, literalistic level of magic consciousness[6]—an incarnate pollution that can be disposed of.

In the Yom Kippur rite there is also a clear sense of the ramifications of confessing sin and atoning for guilt. The Hebrew word for atonement, *kipper,* is related to *kippurim,* eliminatory procedures. There are etymological parallels in both Babylonian and Arabic. A Babylonian rite on the fifth day of the ten-day New Year festival was called *kupperu* and involved purgation, purification, confession of sins and a human sacrifice.[7] The original meaning of the Babylonian word is "to purge or wipe away," suggesting that the blood sacrifice removes the stain of sins. Another derivation based on an Arabic parallel suggests the meaning "to cover." This suggests covering one's guilt, hiding from the eyes of the offended deity by means of reparation.

Jung has defined guilt as the emotion experienced when one feels oneself to have fallen out of the state of wholeness and to be alienated from God, or, in psychological terms, from the Self, the regulating

11

center of the psyche.[8] When the Self is projected onto a collectivity or parent, the guilt will be felt for deviating from their established standards of behavior. Guilt, as an "ever-present . . . component in oneself,"[9] manifests with special poignancy when we feel unacceptable to ourselves, enmeshed in conflicts of duty that divide us and force us to participate in crimes of omission or commission. Such crimes we can neither help nor bear. Ultimately, we may be restored to a sense of wholeness by enduring the conflict and bringing the polarized opposites to consciousness, thus activating what Jung called the transcendent function.[10]

At the time when the Hebrew ritual took its Biblical form, the individual ego was still embedded in the collective, and collective mores (the Law) were just in the process of being codified. This Law, rather than individual conscience, was the source of binding imperatives. It was seen as the sacred gift of a single, patriarchal God who was defined as good and identified with the unity, continuity and perfectability of His Chosen People. In such a situation the restoration of a sense of wholeness, the restoration of a sense of congruence between man and God, depended on a consciousness-fostering ritual separation from evil by collective confession and sacrifice. The scapegoat rite was then adapted from older rites: one exorcising sickness by devoting a sacrifice to the goat god of Semitic herdsmen; the other the yearly ritual death of a human sacrifice to purify and renew the community. The Hebrew ritual became a mode of purging evil and teaching ethical sensitivity. It was included in the New Year festival.

The atonement aspect of the New Year ritual was redefined by the Hebrews. It came to stand in stark contrast to renewal festivals in neighboring polytheistic cultures, where rites of ritual death of the scapegoat Year King and of orgiastic indulgence and sacred marriage reunited the human and divine realms and restored the members of the community to a sense of wholeness through *participation mystique,* a state of unconscious identity with the god.[11] The God of Abraham and Moses stood against such modes of renewal through return to license and the *prima materia* of chaos via ecstatic unity.[12] Yahweh demanded the ordered riddance of defined negative elements. As these were laid on the scapegoat's head, the sense of guilt for falling out of a state of oneness with the collective and its shared, sacred values was purged. Again the members of the community could stand purified and united with each other, feeling blessed by their God. The symbolic system of purity and wholeness necessary for the group's survival was restored.

All such riddance ceremonies, however, operate by virtue of expelling what is felt to be alien. Erich Neumann, drawing an analogy between child development and cultural history, relates scapegoat rites to anal rejection. He finds rejection of feces analogous to the repression of shadow necessary for ego consolidation.[13] This suggests the complexity of the motif. What is rejected is initially acceptable to the infant and its caretaker. Excrement is part of what was once nourishment necessary for survival, the inevitable by-product of life and body-ego health, expelled proudly by the child as an expression of the creative capacity to form material life. It is in some cultures considered valuable fertilizer, in others a ritual cleanser. Yet it has traversed the body's boundary and can be considered alien and dirty. As Mary Douglas suggests, dirt is "matter out of place" in "a symbolic system of purity."[14] It is "that which must not be included if a pattern is to be maintained,"[15] for it challenges the status quo. Thus it becomes ritually tabooed, polluting; it carries the idea of danger.

Some human scapegoats identified with the tabooed and alien material were condemned sinners and criminals who earned pardon by accepting the role for the community. They had offended against the moral code. Some were priests who were immune from the contagion with evil, and others were actors who undertook the ritual drama for pay. But even one who for positive reasons did not fit the prevailing norm could be singled out, negatively tabooed and execrated.[16]

Frazer has described human scapegoats chosen because they were ugly or deformed or "given to fits," while others were chosen because they were unusually strong.[17] In Rome, a man representing the blacksmith, Mamurius Veturius, was the scapegoat.[18] And originally the king, who stood outside the cultural order by being both at its center and, as ruler, above it, was the scapegoat of the community.[19] He was made sacred in the ritual through his identity with the Year God, the partner of the Goddess. His sacrifice ensured the foundation of a prosperous new year.

In the Western world this scapegoat role has often fallen onto Jews and other minorities. It may also fall onto girl children and the women they become. These groups have often carried values needed by society as a whole,[20] but values the culture prefers to keep in the shadow. When these values are derogated and the individuals identify with the scapegoat role, they may play out their identification in self-rejection and in behavior motivated by, or covering, guilt and shame.

In all these choices of scapegoat there are expressed the two primary modes by which any culture defines what is unacceptable and to be expelled or repressed. One is more rational and evokes guilt or shame in the transgressor toward the superego (described by Jung as that "consciously acquired stock of traditional customs").[21] The other is less rational and evokes shame toward less conscious but habitual standards of cultural, emotional and aesthetic forms.

Some behaviors seen to be in discord with behavioral and psychological practicality are defined negatively by law and custom. Thus defined they are repressed into the shadow of each individual of that group. There they remain undomesticated and usually unconscious to some degree. Yet when the ego is overcome by an influx of such shadow material, or observes it in another, the experience is often mixed with guilt, anxiety and repressed identification. And fascination, for such attitudes and behaviors represent elements necessary for life which the collective expells—most often by projecting them onto outsiders or specially chosen group members—to maintain a sense of purity and order. Such behaviors are seen as moving against the current of collective evolution at the moment. Yet the community can neither totally purge and repress them, nor can it do without them. It tries to regulate them into modes acceptable to the group (for example, by condoning murder in battle but not within the tribe).

The material felt to be alien varies according to group. To the early Hebrews it was confined to overt infractions of Biblical laws. Where a Christian mode prevails, the legally prohibited behaviors become interwoven in a web of similarly negative motives and intentions. More is repressed, not just the murderous or adulterous actions, but even the angry and lustful emotions. In the primarily patriarchal Judeo-Christian culture this has led to a devaluation of many behaviors (usually branded vicious, selfish or weak); to a devaluation of attitudes and functions not developed by the collective (especially introverted feeling and intuition);[22] and to a devaluation of instinctual appetites and affects, personal sensitivities and rhythms, that the predominant group mores cannot tolerate.

Cultural values, however, are not only defined by codifiable mores. There are also emotional-aesthetic habits which create standards of form and feeling. Members of a community who by a quirk of nature happen to be at variance with these are often branded for no particular action on their part. Like the Ugly Duckling, they are rejected because they offend against the aesthetic norm. They do not fit the acceptable, common pattern.

The Black Sheep

The situation of individuals found unacceptable to the community on aesthetic-emotional grounds is analogous in personal psychology to that of the odd child, the "black sheep," within its family.[23] This child feels aberrant, set apart, tabooed. Such alienation seems to occur at a primal level of experiencing the world both chronologically and in terms of the magic-matriarchal level of consciousness that operates then and persists as a deep stratum in the psyche. The child suffers, as a result of its alienation from the maternal figure, what Neumann calls the "primary feeling of guilt."

> A central symptom of a disturbed primal relationship is the primary feeling of guilt. It is characteristic of the psychic disorders of Western man. . . . This type of guilt feeling appears in an early phase and is archaic; and it should not be confused with, and above all not derived from, the later guilt feelings connected with the separation of the World Parents and manifested in the Oedipus complex. . . . The primary guilt feeling goes back to the pre-ego phase . . . [and] leads the child to associate the disturbance of the primal relationship with its own primordial guilt or original sin.[24]

Individuals identified with the scapegoat archetype feel themselves to be the carriers of shamefully evil behaviors and attitudes that disrupt relationships—that discomfort the parental figure. On the magic-matriarchal level, where part stands for whole, they identify with the stuff branded "wrong" or "ugly" or "bad." The rejection is often enough unconscious, or it is rationalized in superego terms (both by the parent and by the scapegoat), but its roots lie deeper. It is not what the child has done that brings rejection, but what the child is in relation to the parent. The child has been found different and thus threatening and hateful.

The rejection is experienced by the individual as a punishment for being. Guilt, inferiority feelings and a core of ever-present existential anxiety—from the lack of connection to the greater whole—are the individual's burden. This is an underlying guilt toward the Self, projected onto the rejecting family container. The feeling was verbalized by one young man: "What's my sin that they stopped loving me? I feel as if I owe the national debt."[25]

Those identified with the scapegoat archetype also bear an individual guilt compensating their inflation with the archetype, a sense of uneasy fraudulence. This can be seen as guilt toward the individual Self for living in compulsive bondage to a collective role in order to be restored to the redeemed and redeeming community. The bondage that was originally life preserving becomes habitual—something they cannot give up even if they have to sacrifice their own self-assertion and well-being in the attempt to placate or change the collective enough to make their return possible. Thus they remain fixated on the Self in projection on the collective; they cannot find their own inner authority and the integrity of individual conscience.

The combination of these three levels of guilt—to the superego, to the matriarchal level and to the Self—prevents a coherent sense of identity. This underlies the profound sense of "ontological insecurity" (R. Laing's term)[26] that is experienced by schizoid or chronically regressed, scapegoat-identified individuals.

The Hebrew Scapegoat Ritual

In the original Hebrew rite there are two goats and two transpersonal powers. There is also the high priest of Yahweh, who stands as a temporarily consecrated agent of the collective, mediating between the divine and human realms. The preliminary ritual in which the priest atones for himself and his family clearly separates him from his ordinary, albeit priestly, status and allows him to approach safely before Yahweh to perform the Yom Kippur rite. Only then, in the service of God and for the community, does he undertake the fated (by lot) differentiation and dedication of the goats.

One goat is dedicated to Yahweh that He may pardon Israel. It is killed as a sin-offering so that its blood may cleanse and make sacred the sanctuary, tabernacle and altar, the ritual *temenos*. Its blood placates the angry god and atones for "the uncleanness of the sons of Israel, for their transgressions and for all their sins."[27] This goat's remains are treated as unclean and are burned outside the camp. The other goat, the expelled or escaped goat, is dedicated to

Azazel, a chthonic god, later considered a fallen angel by the Hebrews.[28] Over this goat's head the high priest confesses "all the faults of the sons of Israel, all their transgressions and all their sins and lay[s] them to its charge."[29] This living goat is then taken from the camp and sent out into the wilderness—"and the goat will bear all their faults away with it to a desert place."[30]

The blood of the immolated victim atones and purifies. It represents libido that is dedicated and released through sacrifice to expiate sin and to propitiate the offended God. It is the energy of the instincts made sacred to gain a new connection to the spirit, to reconcile the repentent community to their God and the sacred ideals which created and sustained Hebrew culture. The wandering exiled goat removes the taint of guilt. As sin-bearer, it carries the evils confessed over it away from the place of collective consciousness. It represents libido related to what is both necessary and also guilt-provoking, which is therefore "pushed away to the place identified with it"—that is, ritually returned to its origin in the unconscious.[31] It stands for what evoked guilt and was therefore rejected and repressed by the Hebrew code: those instinctual energies and needs that threatened the development of man in God's image, energies of unbridled impulses, particularly sexuality, rebelliousness, aggression and greed—qualities projected onto Azazel.

2

The Structure of the Scapegoat Complex

I have come to understand the psychology of modern individuals identified with the scapegoat complex as a manifestation of a pathological distortion of the archetypal structure of the Hebrew ritual.

There are two factors that underly this distortion. First, as pointed out in the introduction, there has been a secularization of the originally vital archetypal image, and hence a loss of conscious connection to the sacral matrix from which healing and life-renewal flow. Secondly, there has occurred a radical change in the image and idea of Azazel, which has debased him and caused the libido dedicated to him to be rigidly split off from consciousness, not simply suppressed. This change has also caused splits between the originally united parts of the archetypal pattern.

Both these factors together have broken up the unitary, transpersonally based structure of the archetypal field. Thus the energies symbolized by the images cannot interconnect. As W.B. Yeats put it in *The Second Coming:*

Things fall apart; the centre cannot hold;
Mere anarchy is loosed upon the world,
The blood-dimmed tide is loosed, and everywhere
The ceremony of innocence is drowned.[32]

In the modern scapegoat complex, the energy field has been radically broken apart. I will discuss the particular forms, combinations and modes of operation of the split-apart aspects of the image. While the vectors between the aspects of the image are not necessarily clear cut within each individual case, keeping the whole gestalt and its modern distortions and splits in mind helps to orient the therapist. This is important since much of the process is on a pre-ego, magic level, involving undifferentiated and yet characteristically split energy fields and reactions that enmesh both patient and therapist and resist consciousness.

Azazel, the Accuser

Originally Azazel was a goat god of pre-Hebraic herdsmen. Even in the Biblical rite he is not an opponent of Yahweh, but represents a stage in the repression of a pre-Yahwistic nature deity. He was connected to the feminine, to sensuous beauty and to nature religions. It was said by the later Jewish patriarchs that he led women to sin by teaching them to make cosmetics, and men to war by teaching weaponry.[33] Thus he was connected to erotic and aggressive instinctuality.

Azazel has been translated as "the goat that departs" and "hard rock," or "strong one of God."[34] A Midrash states, "The sins are sent to Azazel so that he may carry them."[35] Clearly no human carrier is capable of this feat. And this is the image corresponding to the original intent of the Biblical ritual where guilt-evoking libido was sent to its transpersonal source. The Hebrews were sufficiently aware of their instinctual impulses that they could enforce responsible suppression. Thus in the ritual they consciously and reverently sent to the chthonic god those sins men could not carry.[36]

Increasingly, however, Azazel came to carry the projection of one side of Yahweh. Historically this permitted the image of Yahweh to begin to be differentiated from those primitive nature gods of sheer power and creativity:

> Yahweh was capable on the one hand of destructive fury, but also of compassion and fidelity. He was, therefore, in a sense a symbol in transition, from the images of savage gods of primitive men to that of the "loving god" to be elaborated in later centuries.[37]

Increasingly Azazel came to bear the defensive exaggeration of Yahweh's own reaction against the world of the feminine and the pre-Hebraic nature gods. He himself became Yahweh's scapegoat, and was redefined as a rebel angel, simplified, made opposite and evil in order to excise Yahweh's shadow. The old god was made into demon.

The image of Azazel changed as the split between good God and devil became deeper. Ginzberg tells the Jewish legend that Azazel, the demon to whom the escaped goat was sent, was once an angel who accused Israel before God:

> "Why hast Thou Mercy on them when they provoke Thee? Thou shouldst rather destroy them." And God replied, "If thou wouldst be among them thou wouldst also sin." Whereupon Azazel requested to be tested and descended to live among men. An evil impulse overcame him . . .

and he fell into lust. He was punished by being made to live apart from God and men in the wilderness, "to close the mouths of the accusers for they will be warned of his fate and will be silent."[38]

Azazel came then to stand, psychologically, for the arrogantly pure, condemning, supercritical judge who would hold men to a standard of behavior he cannot live by himself, for the instinctive impulse erupts through his brittle discipline. His is a standard that takes no account of the facts of life and the embeddedness of man in nature. It implies contemptuously that, by arrogance and will alone, one can withstand the tests of life.

Azazel, here, has come to be like Satan, the antagonist. As accuser against men, he represents divine Justice separated from divine Mercy, what Gershom Scholem, writing on the Kaballah, calls "the radically evil."[39] He represents the evil of a demonic one-sidedness and splitting, of being swept away by a single pattern of behavior.[40] He becomes the bearer of the evil of divine wrath.

As the Hebrew scapegoat image became distorted, Azazel came to function from this perspective. He became the arrogant, condemning accuser, an upholder of a morality of dogmatic and perfectionistic imperatives, a demonic destroyer of those who would transgress Yahweh's Law. It is this exaggeratedly one-sided, sadistic distortion of the original chthonic deity that changes Azazel into a condemning, scapegoating accuser in the psychology of modern men and women, the antilibidinous superego in sadistic form: raw contempt.

In individuals identified with the scapegoat complex this accuser is constellated by the rejecting behaviors of the family. It derives from the moralistic judgments of the mother or father, which relate, as does the Hebraic Azazel, in terms of how things should be rather than things as they are.

When consciousness is identified with the condemning scapegoater part of the complex, then the individual accuses others, with superior virtue-mongering and righteousness. When consciousness is identified with both victim and demonic scapegoater, the demonic accuser constantly rejects, blames, finds unworthy one's own attitudes and actions, and one masochistically accepts the rejection. When consciousness is identified with both accuser and alienated persona-ego, the accuser holds up collective labels and imperatives which one strives to fulfill while ignoring individual needs—except the needs to be right, to win or succeed, in order to fit in, to belong.

In each case the accusing scapegoater is experienced as a heightened but oversimplified morality which stands for collective virtues, and hence against instinctual life; yet it has the impersonal and compelling force of an instinct. It is perceived as an automatic sneer or accusation, a black and white judgment, an evaluation before even the facts are noted. Thus it functions like a perverted, collectivized, rigid feeling function, untempered by descriptions of reality provided by sensation or intuition. In each case the demonic accuser functions with the arrogated power and authority of the Self, while the person identified with the scapegoat archetype both clings to it and feels terrified before it and before those humans onto whom it is projected. As one woman reported: "I'd be a horror without the Judge, I'd be lazy, selfish, mean, gluttonous. I'd have the seven deadly sins."

This sadistic superego is present in the psychology of individuals identified with the scapegoat even if they consciously identify with the alienated persona-ego or the victim-ego.

The Holocausted Goat

Besides the condemning accuser, there is also the "holocausted goat," originally symbolizing libido sacrificed to the offended Yahweh. In the Hebrew ritual it was energy propitiating God and permitting collective purification and renewal through atoning contact with the transpersonal. In the modern complex, however, this goat corresponds to the hidden, helpless pre-ego or victim-ego, which has suffered and is identified with rejection. It represents libido that has been merely arrested and scattered, or hidden, not made sacred.

Because the victim-ego is unable to live up to collective ideals and is thus unpardonable, it feels unworthy to live. It experiences the "primary feeling of guilt." Rather than making connection to other persons or to the transpersonal, this rejected victim-ego survives in a dead, chronically regressed, undeintegrated or fragmented state. It clings to a secret longing for atonement, renewal and rebirth. But it represents the failure of renewal, for conscious connection to the source of transformation has been lost so early it cannot be found alone. And atonement means only achievement of the collective ideals through destruction of anything less. As one man expressed this:

> My agony and aloneness, my sense of total incapacity, my wish to purify myself with suicide—it's a thirst for renewal, a shedding of these pieces of my old body. A desperate measure, and I get stuck in the destruction over and over, ruining all my projects and relations

because no seed can grow because I have never been good enough, there is no ground I can trust.

This hidden victim-ego feels inadequate to the demands of reality since it cannot claim either its dependency needs or its power without incurring guilt. Thus it lives as if it were an infant before life. In patients' material this infant is often described as "tortured," "deathly ill," or "stony," "an utterly lost waif." One woman's initial dream showed her making a snow bed for her baby, "to keep it safely on ice." Another woman brought a dream in which she was told about a tiny child encased in a lead safe-deposit box. The baby was exhausted, and the dream ego had no key and little desire to try to get it out of storage.

In therapy there is an initial aversion on the patients' part to dealing with the hidden, helpless and victimized child in themselves, for they identify both with its helplessness and also with the rejecting, despising, superego. They thus suffer an incapacitating splitting of consciousness. Yet it is this utterly passive, unconscious and lost part which holds the seed of spiritual renewal and which therapy must find and redeem. The therapeutic relationship can provide a nurturing, organic container in which it can securely grow—grow to find an accepting Self image and a viable new grounded relation to life, initially in the transference and ultimately in the transpersonal.

Since this Self image is projected onto the therapist at first, the transference energy causes the patient to fall into needy love-hate when this victim-ego is finally touched. The therapist is seen as the redeemer of the child, so lost and starved it feels it cannot ever receive enough. Images in dreams and drawings of black holes in space, of devouring, greedy animals and grabbing street beggars are common. The possibility of acceptance in therapy allows the pre-ego to be acknowledged, but the inevitable frustrations by the rituals of therapy, and the human limits and personality of the therapist, stir the old wounds and evoke rage and hatred. It is essential that the therapist accept both the intense needy love and the hatred, for they are the primary initial affects of the victim-ego held so long out of life.

The Wandering Goat

There is also the wandering goat, the chosen and over-burdened carrier of collective guilt. This is analogous to the libido of impulses which originally threatened or challenged the ideals of the status quo and were called sinful. This libido evoked guilt and was banished. As discussed above, it was dedicated to the chthonic Azazel and returned to its place of origin in the unconscious through the conscious ethical responsibility fostered in the Hebrew rite.

In the modern complex Azazel is a condemning judge, not a divine source and carrier. Since he represents a negativized spirit that will not accept or recognize any wayward impulsivity, the wandering goat becomes a symbol of dissociated, hence demonic, energies that have lost their connection to a transpersonal, neutral libido source. They cannot find the matrix in which they can be put to rest, and they cannot be admitted into consciousness at all while the sadistic accuser controls what is acceptable.

These energies are the split-off aggressive, sexual and dependency needs that erupt impulsively and compulsively in the schizoid individual and are experienced with frightened awe and guilt when they are not denied completely. Since these impulses cannot find their transpersonal ground, they stay attached to the scapegoat-identified individual as if they were his or her personal burden. They force the development of a precocious and grandiose persona-ego which feels duty-bound to carry them. This provides some sense of positive identity and an enormously grandiose strength compensating the fragility and masochism of the victim-ego. To be the "Strong One of God" is felt to be the scapegoat-identified individual's role.

In the absence of other caretaking, this alienated and precociously duty-ridden persona-ego serves as defense for the victim-ego. It ensures that the fragile victim will be kept safely "on ice," with a determination that ensures its living, albeit in hiding.

The Priest and the Persona-Ego

Because the potency of the divine has been secularized and distorted, the figure of the priest no longer stands for a reverent collective consciousness. It has come to represent not the voice of an offended but merciful God, but the voice of the secular collective that has lost its connection to the inner world and to spirit.

Anywhere, not just in the purified ritual *temenos,* the priestly voice sets forth what is considered good with the authority once vested in the transpersonal. And it serves, without special consecration, as a model of what is collectively acceptable. Thus, in the scapegoat complex, the false priest colludes with the accuser to force a quality of persona adaptation alienated from the inner world and functioning only with external, necessarily unintegrated, maskings. This priest is analogous to the parental and collective voices which define what is good or ideal. These become the teachers and models for the alienated persona-ego with which the scapegoat-identified individual attempts to hide the shadow material he or she is identified with and "chosen" to bear.

The alienated persona-ego learns to function in the world with varying degrees of success, adapting to external circumstances. It seeks its identity outside itself, attempting to meet the Self in projection upon others, and to find the acceptance that its role of sin-carrier and shadow-bearer inevitably prevents.

Indeed, the shadow-carrying, alienated and wandering ego longs so for an accepting collective that it will adopt any persona. It will placate, ingratiate, clown, become indispensably competent, sell its soul, to belong to whichever collectives are valued—even as it is resigned to being an outcast and without the right to protect itself directly. It walks condemned in the wilderness of Azazel, covering its negative inflation with proud and passive stoicism, often with a sense of righteous martyrdom. It feels its special polluted burden, convinced that no one can accept it unless it performs agreeably and well.

The persona-ego cannot trust and cannot find a value system higher than that of the condemning accuser. It hides the collective shadow material with which it feels identified beneath its multiple roles and façades, wandering precariously, habituated to rejection and longing for release. But it also fears acceptance, for that would mean laying down the burden upon which its identity rests. An exile outside the boundaries of the original community, it lives with makeshift collective containers that mediate the transpersonal forces and keep the individual from falling directly into the terror and richness of the unconscious. For, unlike the psychotic, the scapegoat-identified person is related to reality through this persona-ego and may even fulfill role adaptations successfully, although with a driven urge to competence.

Generally this shadow-carrying, alienated ego with nothing to rely on but persona is met early in therapy. One of the problems at this stage is both to tolerate its necessary presence as the only mediator in relationship and to avoid its attempt to come to some agreeable, superficial collusion with the analytic container. As one man put it:

> I'm always moving the scenery so it looks good to the audience. I thought you would like it if I played up being an intellectual and poetic. My last therapists did. I thought I could string you along. Now I don't know what to do. It's a relief, but also humiliating and frightening—like being in no man's land, exposed and vulnerable.

Here the mixture of desire for acceptance and uneasy power in relation to the therapist are clear. So, too, is the value of makeshift personae to protect and to ward off having to deal with the helplessness of the victim-ego in the face of expected superego condemnation. Until the therapeutic bond can be trusted, and until dreams suggest the patient can bear confrontation, such personae need to be endured. Premature confrontation and interpretation can destroy a growing trust and wall off the victim-ego with a seeming adaptation and cooperation that is only another defense.

3

Exile in the Wilderness

To wander in the wilderness has always been an awesome image; yet such exile is basic to the myth of Western man since the Fall, that rupture of an initial bond and harmony which is analogous to a loss of paradise and birth into earth's difficult separations and struggles. Exile is an archetypal image of the painful stimulus that forces individuals to seek for return and atonement with the transpersonal.

For most people, the wilderness is a place beyond the accepted cultural forms, filled with "the potency of disorder . . . in contact with danger . . . at the source of power."[41] In the wilderness the individual confronts the transpersonal, the unknown. When entered consciously and willingly by a shaman-healer or prophet, the wilderness experience can convey special vitality, special powers and authority; and those powers and the consciousness gained from the transpersonal source can be brought back to enrich the collective.[42] When entered unwillingly as a condemned alien, like Cain or Ishmael or the scapegoat, the desert is a curse.

To scapegoat-identified individuals, the wilderness is an image expressing their existential experience of profound alienation and exile. It is the world of their own perceived reality that encompasses them, for they feel anomalous, outside the collective borders, beyond acceptance. Without a supportive internal figure, they are cut off from transpersonal and collective sustenance unless they are temporarily identified with an acceptable persona role. The wilderness thus seems an arid and overpoweringly immense wasteland, a place of dazed confusion and misery. It is the terrible Azazel's domain.

Psychologically for these individuals, the wilderness is analogous to their sense of paralyzed apathy, meaninglessness and abandonment-panic. It mirrors the pain of their never-belonging, of homelessness, of living in hiding. They feel seen when this is interpreted as a sense of living in hell or in the underworld all their life, for they have experienced no internal safety and no outer holding. It is paradoxically also the place of their eventual reunion with the hidden individual Self. But since they lack the maternal and collective validation which would create an individual focus of consciousness

26

and will, they can only initially dwell in unfocused chaos, unable to make contact with the potencies of the source except through terror or omnipotent identification.

Because they feel radically unacceptable, their unmet longing has as unmediated archetypal flavor. Their exile is marked by an intense hunger for connection with both personal and transpersonal Other, even a palpable appetite for the divine. Yet it is also marked by a profound fear of all connection. This keeps the appetite intensely and torturously alive. They are filled with the craving to belong to a stable, predictable, containing reality where a modicum of ego control and invulnerability would protect their fragility from the onslaughts of unmediated transpersonal energies. Instead, they live with an omnipresent sense of danger and an awareness of the shadow that others around them do not wish to see. They may even long for death as an end to their sense of exile, or have a strong sense they should never have been born.

Such a state was expressed by one young woman in analysis. When she was no longer able to function by means of her competent but brittle scientist's persona, she withdrew, staying in bed, crying that nothing had ever made sense, that she hated life and wanted to be cared for, that she had to be her unhappy family's "savioress," that she was "a horrible, dead doll-baby whose eyes had fallen inside her head." She felt chaotically fragmented, identifying simultaneously with several parts of the complex: the victim-ego, the redeemer, the accuser and the persona-doll. For some time she could not perceive or act except from within the complex.

Another scapegoat-identified woman after beginning analysis began to experience insomnia, a symptom which surprised her, for she had initially enjoyed the sleep that brought dreams fruitful for her analytic work. Worrying about her new problem, she had a dream that she was to take an examination to purify her system. It involved submersion in a liquid until she lost consciousness. She then experienced herself awake in a world ruled by a werewolf named Richard the Third. It was clear that she experienced the initiatory ordeal that permits change of consciousness (sleep and therapy and the examination) as the purification which returned her to the dreaded underworld-wilderness in which she had lived most of her life. Its ruler was a powerful monster tyrant, and her habitual stance was terror and masochistic submission to its perfectionistic force. She realized that sleep's altered state signified return, via a twisted dialysis, to that suffocating world. Softening her usual defenses and compulsive competence in therapy, she now feared to be captured again by the twisted demonic ruler of her family's cruel superego. She was also beginning to project this perfectionistic imperative into the analysis, trying to second-guess the therapist in order to be a good and interesting patient.

After she began a more conscious confrontation with the force of these images in her past and present life, the symptomatic insomnia lifted. Then she dreamt of an ally whose hand she held as she crossed a dry culvert. The watery unconsciousness had dried up, and she now had an inner figure with whom she could enter and cross the wilderness. Accepting her own perfectionism and tyranny was, of course, not yet at issue; and such an interpretation would then have been premature, for her ego was not yet strong enough to take responsibility for such shadow energies. It was enough at this stage to point out how she had been victimized.

Omnipresent in the wilderness is the accusing scapegoater. It rejects from every direction, accusing one of being a freak in seeking help, of being incapable of using help, of being different and of being unable to change. The individual thus fears that the pain of rejection is everywhere. The therapist needs to deal carefully with the fear in order to foster trust and to build ego consciousness and strength. Initially, this means allying oneself with the patient's fragmented sense of identity against the demonic accusing Azazel, pointing out the attack and sometimes even taking a protective or assertive role until adequate self-protective skills can be learned through modeling. It means accepting the paranoia and defenses in order to make them conscious. In many cases it also involves entering the wilderness empathically and sometimes amplifying the patient's sense of despair with material expressing comparable misery. Such amplification serves to assuage the patient's utter loneliness with a sufficiently impersonal mirror not to threaten his or her identity based on being a "loner." Occasionally, however, such amplification may frighten the patient, as when it is taken to imply the therapist's agreement with the internal accusing scapegoater that such misery is, indeed, the true state of the world.

Even a simple descriptive statement can be distorted into a seeming collusion with the sadistic accuser. Since what is most real is the negative judgment of habitual self-contempt, even an objective remark can be distorted to split the therapeutic alliance and to repeat the patient's compulsion to remain in familiar, though painful, exile. Conversely, the therapist's empathy can cause the patient to see the therapist as just another scapegoat-victim, too wounded or weak or weird to provide good therapy. The splits of the complex distort much interpretation at first, and both the accuser's contempt and the victim's fear regularly threaten to spoil the potential of the analytic relationship. One woman eventually realized she wanted the analyst to contradict her litany of gloom so she could dismiss the analyst's position as too positive and infantilizing.

Throughout, interpretations need to be carefully balanced, for the complex's impulse to polarize is not only counterproductive but adds to the patient's loneliness. Since the reality of the "hellish" exile is denied by the collective, which does not want to see its shadow, the therapist will be tested again and again for the capacity to stay with the patient in surroundings that seem awful, and yet neither polarize against the painful reality nor merge with the pained one. The therapist will be tested for the ability to "survive."

The wilderness is similar to the wasteland in its implication of aridity. In the wilderness there can be only a distorted relationship, if any at all, to inner creative flow. When caught in the scapegoat complex an individual cannot bear the solitude necessary for original creative work because solitude then implies only desolation or defiant alienation. Having to know, and compulsive self-accusation, prevent gestating anything original. Scapegoat-identified individuals are focused not on their own creative source but on defensive service to the ideals of the collective and on their own incapacity and rejectability. Thus within the complex the individual is entitled access to the imaginal only in solipsistic secret or stolen safety. By never sharing their creative efforts, they are safe from expected spoiling. By stealing from another's forms to produce for the audience what it has already appreciated, they are also safely protected from the accuser's scorn projected onto the audience. The perfectionism of the inner scapegoating accuser clogs the improvisational play necessary for finding one's own voice. And while its high standards may aid in the acquisition of disciplined work habits, and may help one accomplish standardized or assigned chores, they are counterproductive for tasks requiring creativity, the expression of the originality of the individual Self.

When the creative channels open, it is a sign that the grip of the complex has loosened. Finding such expressive channels is a necessity for those identified with demonic energies, as scapegoated individuals are. The creative form provides a vessel for the containment and taming of those energies.

4

Scapegoating within the Family

There is currently considerable clinical literature relating the carrying of the scapegoat role within the family context to severe pathology.[43] Through identification with the scapegoat role, aspects of ego development are inhibited at the oral stage. Further, the archetypes of ego development are skewed toward that of the alienated, fragmented, passive victim and the compensatory roles of suffering servant and savior. Instinctive energies are not tamed or integrated; they remain split, eruptive and frightening. The adult scapegoat's inability to develop a personal identity and self-confidence is due to having been burdened very early in life with those elements devalued, denied, repressed and dissociated by the parents, who initially represent the collective.

Since there is no conscious mode of purgation—except scapegoating others, especially racial and ethnic minorities—our modern secular culture offers little help in dealing with shadow material. Thus the problem has fallen into unconsciousness. The shadow is projected and operates through unconscious complexes.

The family of the scapegoat-identified individual is generally concerned enough with the external aspects of collective morality to need to purge itself, as though its members were defensive before some ancestral or societal emphasis on being good, or at least appearing to be. They cannot process what they consider negative, or discriminate actions from actor. The parents and others who scapegoat in this modern, unconscious way are of course themselves caught in the scapegoat complex. But their ego identity is often closer to those parts of the complex I have been calling the demonic accuser and the priest. They tend to have very strong superego standards, and often strive to be pillars of the community: ministers, doctors, professors, politicians, psychologists. They have an aggressive and vested interest in a persona image that fits with collective standards of virtue and good form, for their identity is ultimately dependent on collective and external validation. But they seem able to find enough of this to remain unconscious of aspects of themselves which could not be thus validated. Their denial of personal shadow dissociates them from their instinctual depths and individuality and makes them brittle and defensive. Others, including their children, can sense their fragility and denied shadow and may react by over-protecting them or attacking their hypocrisy.

Generally the parents of scapegoat-identified individuals have conveyed to their children that they—the parents—are both fearful of and incapable of confronting emotional and symbolic reality. They put roles, practicalities and imperatives—impersonal issues—as buffers between others and themselves. Propriety and duty supplant personal feeling and responsibility in relationships. They fear the exposure, the nakedness, of direct emotional contact. (Anxiety meant to one patient's mother a sign of lack of sleep; to another patient's parents a grateful "thank you" meant merely that the gift had arrived.) Coping competently is a primary value, and emotions expressing pain and fear are belittled or ignored.

Scapegoaters seem to have a profound fear of confronting their own essential helplessness before life. They defend against this helplessness by acting concretistically, as if there were a practical solution to every problem. Within the complex and in relation to the scapegoated child they are stuck themselves in magical concretistic thought. The reality of the psyche is not admitted. It is split off. Thus they tend to read emotional messages as concrete, collective, practical signs, misinterpreting the child's affect as a physical fact, a concrete demand or a globalized statement. These concretizations and globalizations exacerbate feelings of helplessness, which scapegoaters, with their brittle persona-egos, cannot tolerate. Hence they are thrown into deeper cycles of rejecting the seemingly too potent child.

In cases where emotional reality is admitted by the scapegoating parents, it is found acceptable only in particular, collectively sanctioned modes of expression. "When we talked about our feelings maturely and endlessly, so she could feed off them, then we could say we were angry or upset," said one young woman about her mother's demanding style of psychologizing. In most cases the scapegoating parent receives the child's expression of impulses so defensively and so impersonally that the child feels their danger to the adult—and hence also to itself. Shadow material cannot, in such a situation, be humanly mediated.

Furthermore, from under the brittle, collectivized persona the denied parental shadow impulses often erupt irresponsibly in the "safety" of the home. Alternatively, or as well, they may be seen in projection and then contemptuously attacked. One scapegoat-identified man beginning to be aware of his schizoid core expressed this picture:

> My parents either ignored what they thought evil—including their violent rages—or else they tried openly to destroy it with mockery. I felt most of myself was unseen and endangered, and I learned not to risk revealing my personal reactions. Getting loved meant giving out what was approved, safe. The real me lived in hiding.

Anthropologist Mary Douglas puts this man's remarks in a larger perspective:

> There are several ways of treating anomalies. Negatively we can ignore, just not perceive, or perceiving we can condemn. Positively we can deliberately confront the anomaly and try to create a new pattern of reality in which it has a place.[44]

Such a positive confrontation with what is apparently out of place—shadow material—is rare enough in our culture, but it is impossible for scapegoaters, who fear to open the pattern of their reality beyond what they feel the collective sanctions. The scapegoating parents are invariably themselves the fragile and wounded children of righteous, demanding parents, and they have no stronger sense of a Self which validates their wholeness than their scapegoated children can have.

The dark shadow side—the guilt-laden material that cannot be tolerated by the parents—is thus left as a potent part of the unconscious environment. The scapegoat-identified adult, usually by nature especially sensitive to unconscious and emotional undercurrents, and often involved in a helping profession, was the child who picked up and carried the family shadow. Often there is a particularly strong unconscious bonding with the scapegoating parent, sometimes verbalized as a feeling that that parent needed or wanted the child's care. Part of this may be projection of the child's own unmet need, but part is objective assessment of the unmet parental need. Such bonding makes expressions of hostility difficult, not only because of the danger of abrupt defensive retaliation, but also because the parent's dependent shadow was and is so often palpably present to the child/adult. "I couldn't hit her; she was already down, too . . . I'm just like her—a tyrant and a phoney and a bitch and a wreck," one woman said of her mother, verbalizing her nascent awareness of the splits caused by the complex and the fact that she and her mother both suffered it, albeit from different perspectives.

This bonding, also, is a mark of *participation mystique,* the symbiotic field in which scapegoat and scapegoater exist on the magic level of consciousness. Within this field psychic contagion (or "projective identification") is a fact. Jung has written of the possibility of catching even a bad conscience due to the psychoid nature of the archetype.[45] Scapegoat-identified individuals are those who habitually caught the bad conscience, perceived the denied shadow and felt responsible for it. They became hypersensitive to ethical and emotional issues and accepted the role of tending, by empathy and nurturant caretaking, the shadow qualities in others.

Sometimes the scapegoated individual is cast in the role of the family sick member. Alternatively, when the parents also repress dependency needs, she or he may be seen as the family's envied and most responsible member, whose needs as well as individuality are overlooked—even spoiled. In both cases the individual comes into therapy with a self-description of feeling like a criminal, invalid, pariah, leper or freak. Basic is the sense of isolation and guilt—a terrible foretaste of individuality from the position of the rejected and exiled one.

5

The Scapegoat Complex and Ego Structure

In the field of psychology the taking in of needs is equated with orality, while the willful assertion of one's own formed emotional stuff is related to anality.[46] From personal histories it is clear that oral wounds are not necessarily suffered only at a very early age. Seen symbolically as the need to grasp, take in, possess, this set of behaviors can be wounded not only by conflicts and deprivations related to eating and receiving affection and appropriate mirroring attention, but also by any hurt or taboo against phase-appropriate selfishness or possessiveness even if suffered up to, say, ages five to seven. Such wounding brings a feeling of deprivation and the existential sense of being unworthy to receive. The feeling of unworthiness may also come about through assimilating, by psychic contagion, the caretaker's sense of incapacity to give physically or emotionally. Similarly, any undue prohibition concerning elimination or aggression can create a wound in the area of self-assertion.

Being caught in the scapegoat complex affects 1) perception and consciousness, that is, how one sees and forms experience; 2) the ability to contain and endure suffering; 3) one's capacity for self-assertion; and 4) the capacity for need gratification.

These four modalities of functioning can perhaps be related to basic developmental phases, but on a symbolic rather than a psychosexual level. Scapegoat-identified individuals have particular kinds of experience in each modality, depending on the combinations of the complex and their own talents and sensitivities.

Distortions of Perception

We see the basics of perceptual patterning in the early awakening of the senses and the experiences which stimulate them within a range of tolerable comfort. Individuals who are overstimulated by parental needs or who are especially sensitive by nature, may perceive both pain and pleasure intensely. And because such experiences have not been humanly mediated, the individual tends to remain fixated at the early, magic levels of perception and intensity.

Such persons may easily seem anomalous to others in their environment. Not uncommonly they are perceived by the scapegoating parents as dangerous viewers of shadow material best left unseen. Like the child who saw that the emperor's fabled robe was imaginary, their vision often pierces the persona because it is attuned to the deeper layers of the psyche. Because they arouse unconscious discomfort, their perceptions may be disregarded or denied, while they themselves are shamed and rejected, made to feel a dis-ease comparable to that aroused in those they seem to see through. This may occur even in infancy when the parent suffers the fear of being found out. As one woman reported:

> My mother turned me away or averted her own eyes. She still can't stand to be seen by me, because she thinks I see through her. I don't know if I always did, but she says it started when I was nursing. My being threatened her, forced her to see her own lack.

Here the terrible aspect of the Self (the "eye of God") is projected onto the child, who is feared as carrier of unobtainable ideals. From within the complex, the Self is seen as Azazel, the accuser, by the mother who feels herself imperfect. Such a mother cannot then bear to relate intimately to the infant, for the child's gaze exacerbates her own unconscious scapegoat victim. And the complexes of the parents are passed on for at least the proverbial seven generations, where the archetype behind the complex remains both so unconscious and potent within the culture.

The effect of such seemingly medial sensitivity in the child and the parental projection hung on it was poignantly expressed by a scapegoat-identified man:

> I feel guilty for seeing evil because no one else does. Then either I go crazy or feel I am bad to see someone else as bad when that person says he or she is good . . . It's like a punishment for seeing itself . . . As a child I would—just by seeing and naming—lose any parents I could truly value, who could admit their own humanness, not be hypocrites. And they would shame me, hate me for seeing them. Or they would ignore me and deny that I could see . . . Sometimes I can't trust my perceptions at all.

A related confusion comes about as the result of an empathic bond with the abusive but also beloved parent. Then evil is not seen with sufficient objectivity, and scapegoat-identified individuals may thus approach intolerable situations unaware, or as if magically protected by still childlike naiveté. They may indeed find such situations fascinating and be compelled to return to abuse in order to try to discover the good parent which might be redeemed there. One man expressed this distortion: "He was my father. No one told me it was awful when he attacked us or mother. No one talked to me, so I still usually assume things are okay." He had become involved in submission to a dangerous authority figure he found only "intriguing" and "like my family." He could not see the frivolity of his attitude or the objective reality of danger until a dream presented him with a stark image: "There is a razor blade broken into the jam I am spooning up. It belongs to X."

From inside the complex, reality is perceived through a distorting rigidity that equates consciousness and judgmentalism. What is, is never neutral; it is always good or bad. And so, indeed, Azazel's realm, that place to which the escaped goat is sent, is a bleak landscape of automatic, oversimplified ideas and definitions about how things should be—thoughts that are like judgments. These change like sand dunes without ego participation, according to whatever collective, partial and negatively critical evaluations can be made of the situation. The vitality that comes through an eye that will describe and experience objectively, that can see and accept the whole, is lost.

Two dream images expressing this negatively viewed reality were brought by patients. In the first the dreamer was on trial before a judge like her grandfather. In the dream he wore a permanently fixed black monocle over his only eye. In reality this woman could only define herself negatively, with reference to ideals she fell short of achieving. The second dreamer found that her task was to race across a room stepping only on the black squares of the checkerboard floor. She ran again and again and always lost, since the floor changed as she moved.

Such negatively focused evaluation creates a radical perceptual distortion. Another image from a woman's dream shows how this functions: "I am on a kind of battlefield. There is an arc of lights, but the lights are guns—machine guns to hit some target ahead of me. I am in the line of fire." Here the light of consciousness comes from the same mechanical source as destruction. The woman simultaneously perceived and criticized herself. This made her afraid of perception. She feared to see. She also feared therapy, because to her it meant becoming aware of "terrible things—the devil, the wolf and the west wind." She tried to leave analysis many times until the "terrible judge" was consciously confronted, at which point she could differentiate objective perception from death-dealing criticism.

As the analysis progressed, she began to use her imaginal eyes and could see that those three initial terrors referred to her devilish but valid selfishness and assertion, her wolfish and powerful appetite for life, and her capacity to relate to the "west wind"—the spiritual dimension and her own mortality and immortality. But at first these images could only be viewed negatively from the perspective of rigid, collective judgmentalism and her own fear.

Another person with a severe scapegoat rejection complex began slowly to realize that his accuser functioned from within and was projected onto others. His image shows how the partial yet binding evaluations inhibited him:

> It is as if there were a computer with many slots to catch the print-out cards. There is always a set of ideals that must be achieved: in work, the brilliant, committed genius; in conversation, David Niven; in virility, Sean Connery; in music, Heifetz, etc. The slots under those ideals stop the cards, evaluating my actions as inadequate, weak, too emotional, bad. No card gets through, so I hide my reactions unless it's an area where the computer has no standard, so I don't have to care.

The perfectionist ideals mentioned here are part of the accusatory aspect of the scapegoat complex. Like Karen Horney's "Tyranny of the Shoulds,"[47] they represent those abstract tyrannical standards which are codified as models of persona behaviors; imperatives that, in this case, can no more be reached than can Azazel's impossible ideal of total virtue. Yet it is against them that every personal action or attitude is seen as falling short; so the rejection persists, and the individual is forced further and further into self-rejecting isolation. Those identified with the scapegoat archetype have little or no trust in the validity of their own direct perception of facts, affects, thoughts or hunches. Instead, they are habituated to giving credence to multiple, fluctuating, collective evaluations. Until these disparate, perfectionistic ideals are transformed by being related to one limited, whole individual, scapegoat-identified individuals seek to fulfill a multiplicity of disparate persona goals that usually do not at all take their own talents and capacities into account.

Basically there seem to be two gods and two value systems. Scapegoat-identified individuals feel judged according to the condemning ideals and standards of the internal accuser. They are inevitably miserable and guilty, identified with falling short and being bad or wrong. Yet they judge others by the standards of the saving redeemer and "understand" them to the point of sentimentality. They forgive in others exactly the same sins and shortcomings they feel to be despicable in themselves. Justice and Mercy are separated. Azazel (and the later god of the last judgment) and Christ, the accepting son of Jehovah, rule different areas. But both are unconscious. This makes it hard for the ego to coalesce. It can jump back and forth between the perceptual splits without feeling the inconsistencies of the double standard, yet double-bound by them nonetheless.

This double standard is one of the roots of both the confusion and the masochistic self-hate characteristic of the complex. One woman expressed this:

> The only way I have of seeing evil is to see it as me. I am not allowed to see it as part of anyone else. When I looked at my mother's abuse and made an appropriate response, I remember she said it was all me. And I needed an identity after all. I took on that of the bad one.
>   . . . For example, I can easily image myself as a torturer, with all those cruel feelings. It's even an effort to see that isn't how I act. But I can't bear to see someone else as a torturer or anyone hurt. When I turn the torturer feelings into self-hate, at least that way I don't hurt anyone or get punished for turning them against others. The trouble is I have no way of affirming my value except as one capable of any evil. And I'm always confused about what's me and what isn't.

She both defended against her rage by turning it against herself, and felt the compensatory, awful and grandiose power of her identification with evil. This woman provided an example of the typical but unusually profound perceptual confusion in her description of her mother: "She was so strict. I was always out of order and wrong and incompetent. She did the best she could for me, bless her. I am incorrigible." Her perception was split into two separated value systems. For a long time she could not see that she had experienced an ambivalent woman, a personification of the negative and positive aspects of the mother archetype. Her mother was only good, and she was only bad. Her mother's destructive power was always forgivable; even acknowledging that "the strictness" had made her unhappy was a sign of her own "incorrigibility."

This form of distorted perception derives from the automatic oversimplifications of black and white judgmentalism on the magic level of consciousness. One woman described this perceptual splitting as her "necessary ledger system." All experience was labeled for her as good or bad, "either one or the other." So habituated was she to this rigid mode she could not describe or reflect on her experience. At a point when the inadequacy of this mode began to become conscious, she dreamt: "I am trying to find the exact center of a litmus paper. I am using prussic acid to dip the piece into." She associated to this dream:

> Litmus paper can only tell you if something is acid or alkaline. In the dream I focus on it, I don't care about the stuff I am using to divide the two halves. It's like making an either-or judgment. But prussic acid is very dangerous. It's a poison the Nazis used in the death showers, and they divided people to left or right, to die or to work as slave labor.

Her tendency to split the sensing instrument with fanatic, destructive rigidity was dangerous to her, but she was so intent on the precision of the oppositional split that she needed the dream to make her conscious of that fact.

Seeing only the shadow or even identifying with it is a preliminary and polarized mode of honoring wholeness in a family that splits off its own shadow and identifies with the good. By accepting the negativity the scapegoat-identified individual ensures that it can no longer be denied with fraudulent personae and "positive thinking." Caught within the family complex, the scapegoat serves wholeness and objective reality, albeit by exclusively honoring the rejected parts. It is a terrible calling, to be "a living darkness," as one man called it; yet it is served with passionate integrity until the Self's acceptance and valid wholeness can be experienced through the transference or projected onto other Self figures in the person's life.

When both sides of the polarization are mirrored back, the scapegoat-identified individual initially cannot assimilate any positive value. There is a taboo against it due to the long habit of identification with the guilty, incompetent, rejected one. This "loyalty" is extremely difficult to sacrifice even when there is some experience of positive shadow qualities that might coalesce into an empowered ego. For there is also the integrity that refuses to abandon an aspect of wholeness—the valid horrors and pains of reality to which the scapegoat was devoted by the collective that sought to deny them.

Such demonic splitting into either-or oppositions carries over into personal relations. It can be clearly seen in the transference in the many ways the patient attempts to polarize with the therapist. Sometimes the patient envisions the therapist as all good and the patient as all bad. This fosters the demonic illusion that one can be all-good and without shadow—a goal which might be reached if only the right way is found. This illusion keeps the patient going in a lonely, passive way. To come to sessions can then be addictive—like getting a dose of a drug that maintains the alienated persona-ego's dream of contentment and dulls the pain of feeling lost. But it needs to be interpreted as a defense and seen as an impossible dream before real analytic work can begin.

Such a polarized state of "primitive idealization"[48] was made clear in a woman's drawing in which she and the therapist were represented by figures lying in bed. She added a black halo to the figure of herself and a pink halo to the figure of the therapist. There was also a line down the center of the bed. The drawing made it clear that the therapist was seen in too positive a glow to permit any relatedness except by frustrated longing and the expectation of salvation or rejection. The woman explained, "I have to see you that way because you have to pull me out of my unhappiness." She wanted to stay passive in order to assuage magically her rejected dependency needs. She was willing to wear the black halo, to suffer hopelessness and depression, if the therapist would embody the all-good mother figure. She was willing to carry all the black to maintain her illusion.

In this case an earlier stage of polarization had been pictured in a drawing where the opposites were far separated, with two circles representing herself and the therapist drawn with arrows moving them away from each other. In an intervening stage, the woman had shown herself as a tiny red dot merged in the center of a flower, which she said was the therapist. The flight from relatedness and the womblike containment in a symbol of wholeness had thus changed, in the later drawing of the figures in the bed, to acknowledgment of polarity within a secure relationship. It represented a new stage of developing consciousness.

The typical distortion of perception affects the person's body image in many ways. Generally there is an idealization of some fragment of the acceptable collective image; this becomes the aim and focus of the person's view of his or her own body because it seems to be lacking. "If only I had thicker wrists, I'd be a real man." "If only I weren't so fat, I could flirt and be spontaneous." "If only I had lovely skin, I would feel all right about myself." Marion Woodman has analyzed the psychological consequences of such "addiction to perfection."[49]

Scapegoat-identified persons seize on a particular attribute of their bodies as the cause or justification of their sense of alienation. The thin wrists or obesity or acne is felt to be the one ugly attribute which everyone else notices and despises. It becomes the body counterpart of the scapegoat. The seeming flaw becomes the secret shame, the reason to avoid touch, the felt focus of negative criticism. It becomes the scapegoat's scapegoat on the body level. But it cannot be thrust away. Nor can focus on it be overcome easily, for it is the omnipresent physical concomitant of the complex, a rationalization underlying the self-hatred that is the person's felt identity.

Transference and Countertransference

The scapegoat's habit of carrying the shadow means the therapist must pay particular attention to his or her own shadow material when it comes up in therapy. Conscious acceptance, and often verbal expression by the therapist, is necessary in order not to play into the complex and to provide a model for the responsible handling of individual shadow stuff.

Especially when the patient focuses on a split-off aspect of affect-provoking shadow in self or other and globalizes it to the whole, the therapist needs to stand for both part *and* whole. This allows the analysand's valid responses of fear and anger to a shadow part to be held by an accepting other person. It both curtails denial and helps to heal the splitting many scapegoat-identified individuals have had to use to survive their extreme fear and pain and rage. As one analysand put it, "I want you bigger here and not to get defensive or accept my rage as total. Otherwise, if I bring it in I *am* the spoiler."

Another young woman, who felt many aspects of herself unacceptable, longed for a magic solution that would not involve her in any suffering. At the end of one session I remarked on this wishfulness in a tone that she found hurtful. I agreed with her that my remark was offensive to her, but I did not withdraw it. In the next session she said:

> I was mad at you instead of only hurt, and glad for the way you handled it. You agreed it was offensive, and also had no hard feelings toward me. I would otherwise have felt diminished because I said something offensive. Yet you weren't guilty. It made me feel I could struggle and protect myself and not have to take every piece thrown back at me.

The therapist whose own psychology includes a strong scapegoat complex often fails to differentiate sufficiently his or her own reactions to the patient, and to determine whether these are due to the patient's projected material or to the therapist's own complex. The therapist who feels overly responsible for shadow material in the environment may find it difficult to hold the necessary positive idealizations projected by the patient, and may also assume that the projective affects and images of the patient's psychology belong to the therapist's own shadow. The material may not be recognized as aspects of the patient's process projected onto the analytic situation in order to evoke the patient's habituated rejections and fears, and to ensure the security of old, albeit painful, patterns of relating.

Such repetitions may even come about when the guilty, aggressive or demanding behavior of the patient overloads the therapist and snares him or her into playing out the archetypal, overly-responsible, wandering scapegoat role. Although this may seem to be the opposite of the parental accuser role, the complex itself is thereby reconstituted. As one woman explained:

> You can't be a "guilt-eater" who will make it all right, because then I have to carry you and your positive value and I feel bereft because you don't value you. So I abandon my own feelings in order to care for you as I did with my parents. And I'm responsible again for others and not to my true Self. I don't want that anymore.

This woman was coming to realize her own "guilt-eating" by seeing it in projection on the therapist. Also she was beginning to see the limits of her desire to have the analyst as her good mother. She could begin to mistrust and resist the splits within the complex.

Conversely, therapists with too little awareness of their own shadow and scapegoat complex may tend to deny their own psychological involvement. They may automatically frustrate or deprive the analysand in an attempt to rouse consciousness, ignoring the reality of the victim-ego's needs and not seeing that frustration often tends only to rouse the scapegoat's remarkably subtle and habitual defensive collusion. Or they may unconsciously blame the patient for burdening them and then resent feeling helpless. Coerced by the complex, which spreads its contagion into the analytic field, they may then identify with the condemner or the victim-ego.

Another countertransference possibility arises out of the oppositional splits of the accuser, which posit experience as either good or bad. The patient's tendency to idealize the therapist, as well as the therapist's wish to heal the patient, lead to the constellation of the savior who will redeem the victim—the good mother or father who will make restitution and provide the nurturing experience denied to the outcast. This savior aspect is a potent, but hidden and compensatory, element in the complex (see below, chapter six). Along with unconscious compensatory envy, it needs to be accepted and endured by the therapist—as do all the transference projections—until the patient is ready to grow beyond the containment which the idealizing transference provides. The therapist must bear the projections without identifying with them, knowing that no one can grandiosely atone for the patient's pain by carrying part of his or her fate and history. The therapist's empathy with the analysand, allowing this fate to be seen objectively and suffered through to atonement with the Self, is of far more permanent value.

On the magic level of consciousness the boundary between patient and therapist is constantly in flux. Here the two parties coexist in one symbiotic, synchronistic whole—a uroboric, preverbal, spaceless and timeless *participation mystique*. It may ultimately not matter very much where the psychic boundary is, as long as the therapist can find a personal orientation in the archetypal affect-image field, can see which role she or he is playing out and can disidentify from it.

Acknowledging the mutuality of the scapegoat complex calls the therapist's attention to the uncomfortable pattern in which he or she is partially caught. Working through the complex and disidentifying from it permits coalescing of the pathological split-off parts of the complex. It also permits changing the relationship between therapist and patient, since one party, the therapist, is then freed from the binding unconscious pattern and able to respond with consciousness and concern. On the psychoid-magic level of the transference-countertransference, this is enough to make the necessary space for the curative emotional experience which the patient needs from therapy. (A verbal interpretation may follow at some point, but it is often not essential.)

Containing and Enduring Painful Experience

The capacity to endure discomfort seems to be related to the early experience of touch, to being held intimately and with respect, both in attentive regard and in protecting and containing arms. This gives a child a sense of whole body-Self integrity and identity. The surety of being held within a collective framework maintains this sense. The experience of actual and symbolic holding also permits the pre-ego to learn to suffer and enjoy its own experiences in a strong vessel; they can then be assimilated at phase-appropriate levels.

If the parent is incapable of mediating overpowering emotion and frustration, as most scapegoaters are, or if the caretaker feels a strong taboo against touching or being touched—physically or emotionally—the young child will not feel adequately held. This can lead to uncertainty about the body-ego's ability to resist fragmenting, merging with the environment or being overcome by unconscious forces. The child may then experience debilitating disruptions in its sense of continuous identity.

The sense of having fallen out of touch, of not having or never having had a protective-containing embrace, is central to scapegoat-identified individuals' experience, for they are identified with exile and with only disparate parts of the whole—primarily the shadow parts. They have usually had a problem with bonding and feeling securely held from the earliest weeks, because of the poor psychological "fit" with the parental figure.

In the phenomenology of the scapegoat complex the individual's strengths and reactivity are felt to be the cause of his or her pain, like being a specially selected specimen of goat chosen for sacrifice. This leads to the curious logic that all pain is punishment, that because the individual could pick up the shadow projection, it was deserved. One woman expressed this: "Because I suffer, I know I'm bad. If I didn't feel pain, I'd know I was all right." As a child, she felt she had been held responsible for all misbehavior among her younger siblings. When she got upset at being unjustly accused, she was told her reaction was proof of her guilt. As an adult she continued to equate psychological pain with feeling rejected and inferior.

This equation causes an aversion reaction to the individual's own affect and sensitivity, both because they seemed to be the source of guilt and because they opened the way to feeling more pain. This means no experience can be lived deeply and no relationship to an outer or inner Other can grow, for openness may lead to more suffering. Splitting, denial or unconscious impulsivity are the rule, and ego consciousness cannot develop where there is an automatic evasion of experience. There is often a concomitant atrophy of physical sensation in some areas of the body. There may also be a distortion of body image as well as deep-seated problems connected to assimilating food and eliminating.

Almost invariably there is a body armoring, with varying degrees of rigidity. In the absence of maternal and collective embrace, this armor combines with the persona to hold together the individual's fragmented parts. Inevitably, therefore, some body work is necessary in order to restore a sense of body-Self. Because conscious identity is fragmented and split between part selves or alternating aspects of the complex, one cannot regain a sense of felt wholeness without recourse to the Self latent at the psychoid level of body experience. Touch, sensory awareness and various body therapies can mitigate the lack of experience of holding by an other person or by the body vessel itself.

The power of touch to evoke the whole body-Self in order to process the fragmented parts is remarkable. Sometimes merely laying a hand on the person's arm can provide access to the body vessel. But initially an almost allergic fear of being touched, physically as well as emotionally—and the consequent armoring—make it hard for the patient to stand such a gesture. Armoring also makes it hard for the individual to feel any emotion when functioning in terms of the alienated persona-ego. The most painful tales are told calmly, hence the therapist often has to discover and carry the affect and sometimes give expression to it. The scapegoat-identified individual has built a wall to ward off the pains of the toxic shadow material. This wall serves to isolate the hidden core from further abuse and shame as well as to protect others from the "leprosy" or "radioactive garbage," as one woman called it. "That's my basic nature and I have to keep my distance or keep up a lead shield." Almost all her strength was used in maintaining this guard wall. She had long experience with the fact that her "demonic" energies could not be tolerated by her family and she guarded them to herself.

Yet at the same time the victim-ego is identified with suffering, inflated with the very affect that is avoided. Like the fairytale princess who could feel a pea under dozens of mattresses, all hurts are felt with exquisite sensitivity because they touch the old, raw wounds. There is also identification with the victim in projection and hence a great capacity for surrogate suffering. In this way the victim-ego maintains a connection to its own affects.[50] There tends to be an automatic, almost medial, identification with any sufferer in any situation. But such identification also can evoke fear of the helpless victim-ego's own pain and incapacity to withstand chaos. Then anyone's suffering, or even that of an animal, can lead to generalized panic and flight, or to rage.

All this makes it hard for scapegoat-identified individuals to allow themselves to learn to endure their own discomfort and to evaluate its intensity with any objectivity. There is an automatic assumption that they cannot cope. Thus, when any genuine conflict or anxiety is felt, the individual reacts omnipotently, impatiently and concretely in order to control—to get it removed, undo it, avoid it or fix it up. One said, "I want to be normal. That means I wouldn't feel anything painful." Another said:

> I have to get rid of my feelings. I can't afford them. I can't deal with agony that has no solution, that I can't end.
>
> In my family I felt they always said, "You take it"—so their own pain could go. And that's what I want, too, someone to take it away.

The capacity to witness suffering as an objective fact of life is initially impossible, for the person caught in the scapegoat complex is identified with suffering, grandiosely and negatively inflated, feeling responsible for both its existence and its concrete removal. The victim-ego operates on the magic level of consciousness, literally and concretely merged with the object of feeling or thought. The possibility of being conscious of pain and enduring its sometimes inevitable presence, and yet not identifying with it, does not yet exist.

Where there is an impasse here, it is therapeutically necessary to cooperate with the defenses against the intolerable pain and panic until the analysand can endure them with some confidence that the therapeutic bond will survive. This was effective in the case of a professional woman whose dreams pointed to her taking some responsibility to evaluate and endure. Her habit had been to panic, "like Henny Penny who thought the sky was falling," to "cut out" (leave therapy) and anesthetize herself with heavy doses of medication. This time, while she found a doctor to dose her with tranquilizers, she continued in therapy. Gradually she was able to disidentify from her habitual defensive masochism, that "secret, most real thing I know, terror," to let herself experience raw affect without helpless panic. Through the transference relationship she began to find a different and sturdier reality, as well as a new curiosity which enabled her to witness with wonder her rich variety of emotions. This in turn enabled her to realize that both the therapeutic bond and her own ego container were capable of sustaining her. Thus she could find a different view of her identity and her own courage, and in due course she took herself off the medication.

During this period she dreamt that her therapist had learned to endure the spells of recurrent pain from an old wound with the help of a new-style, holistic medicine doctor who sat by the bed at such times, "patiently knowing what had to be done because it had been before, but not taking the feelings away with any medication or magic." With this new attitude toward affect and pain, she began to feel a shared sense of suffering with another. For the first time she could feel herself emotionally as partner in a human dyad—her first taste of an accepting and companioning community.

The dream image of another woman illustrates the same problem but from a different perspective, for she identified more with the victim-ego: "I am carrying someone who is hurt on my back. It's not as heavy as I might expect. But what a shock to realize it's myself! I am carrying my own self." She had experienced extreme difficulty in the separation-individuation phase of her regression in therapy. She could not easily sacrifice the symbiotic transference, since her personal experience had been of radical exile as soon as she was able to walk. Her parents had at that time been killed in an accident. Although she had received adequate physical care, her grief and need, her rage and its subversion into guilt, had gone untended. These and her defenses against them had enmeshed her in scapegoat psychology. She had carried these overwhelming emotions walled off behind her competent, alienated persona, always overly responsible and cut off from her holocausted core.

Learning to hold her wounded self in a new way was a revelation that allowed this woman to sacrifice the infantile clutching with which the unconscious victimized child in her had compensated her proud alienation. It enabled her to relate as a whole individual, carrying her own wounds and their pain. She could begin to sacrifice her demand for perfect mirroring from the therapist and her family, as she began to sacrifice her demand for restitution of a lost paradise state and to accept the true burden that was her life.

At such a point in therapy, when the transference has survived the repetition compulsion to split the therapeutic bond and recreate the habitual alienation, images for containers of painful experience commonly appear in dreams or drawings. This woman discovered a numinous garbage pail marked with a rose. It symbolized the valued vessel which could hold with feeling her sense of what was unacceptable. Thus her now good-enough ego could disidentify from her habitual role as shadow carrier and throw into the garbage what belonged there. She could trust that the maternal-therapeutic vessel could deal with the garbage.

Another woman at a similar point in her analysis had a dream:

I am in a forest. Suddenly a stag appears and leads me to a clearing.

I see a circle of ancient stones, and the animal paws the ground in
their center. There it makes a hole that goes deep into the earth. It
may have merely uncovered what was there all along.

In active imagination, she wondered what was to be made of the
ancient, sacred opening. Rather than being a tunnel entrance into
the otherworld for herself to explore, she found the stag pushing
refuse left by sightseers into the hole. Meditation on the image
conveyed to her a sense of the transpersonal receptacle of garbage.
It also confronted her with her "sightseer" attitude, one that did not
want to carry her own pain, as her parents had not carried theirs.
The image presented her with an alternative to their scapegoating.
As she put it, "I realize I can put what I cannot deal with myself
into that place—my mother's rejection, my guilts, the pain of X's
death."

Finding such an image furthers disidentification from the
archetypal scapegoat pattern, for it confirms the individual's nascent
sense of being supported both by and beyond the transference. The
image provides an archetypal base for the therapeutic vessel as a
good-enough holding environment. Thus one can forego the need
to be omnipotent and accept that the human dimension does not
have to be capable of handling alone the raw malevolence of reality.
It relieves the ego of the collective and archetypal shadow burden
that had prevented its development.

Having a safe container for painful experiences also makes it
possible to view parental rejection and scapegoating as real abuse.
"I was unfairly dumped on," as one man put it. "I can't carry that
stuff. It's theirs, too." After a period of rage and blame, which help
to consolidate the new, good-enough individual ego but which may
lead to a necessary estrangement from the complaisant scapegoaters,
there may be a new and non-grandiose acceptance of the rejecting
ones. They too may come to be seen as victims, strugglers against
forces with which they had little help. This realization can release
potent, healing affect and a sense of the all-too-human community
of individuals.

There are many amplifications of the transpersonal container of
evil. Among them is Tlazolteutl, the Aztec goddess of childbirth
and "eater of filth," who consumes the sins of men once in each
person's lifetime, just as mother animals often eat the eliminations
of their young to keep the nest clean. There is also the Chinese
smiling Buddha whose fat belly can be rubbed to receive human
pains into it without changing his expression. There is the shaman-

healer's use of raw meat, which is later burned, to absorb sicknesses drawn from patients. In India only Shiva can absorb the lethal poison first produced when the gods churned the Milky Ocean. He could hold it in his throat and not assimilate it totally. Gautama Buddha refused to be a container when the forces of darkness and evil confronted him under the bodhi tree. He conquered them by non-opposition, by being on a meditative, non-polarized plane.

In the Christian tradition there is Christ as Agnus Dei, the Lamb of God sacrificed to bear the sins of mankind. There is also the ritual of absolution of sins granted after confession by the Church, which stands as representative of Christ and thus itself becomes a transpersonal container. Other amplifications are discussed in Frazer's material on the scapegoat.[51]

Often the intolerable affects of the scapegoat-identified patient are felt intensely by the therapist—either empathically or, later, by projective identification when the patient's schizoid defenses are loosened and emotion can flow into the therapeutic vessel. The therapist's own complexes will resonate with the dark wounds and toxins—hate, greed and rage—of the patient's psychology. Working with scapegoat-identified individuals will thus confront the therapist with the need to overcome old polarizations, to avoid concreteness and premature impatience, and to endure strong discomforts without retaliation. The schizoid core of the therapist will inevitably be touched to provide the possibility of consciousness. If the old habits of the therapist's own scapegoat complex can be suffered without undo identification and acting out, genuine healing may occur in both parties.

The Chosen Victim

The "chosen one" in cultures magically practicing sacrifice is iden-tified with the divinity. The victim serves a transpersonal, atonement purpose that is felt to be essential for the sustenance of the group's life and well-being.[52]

Historically, individuals chosen for the scapegoat sacrifice seemed to acquiesce in their role. Often they willingly undertook it out of a profound sense of *participation mystique* (identity with the collective and its transpersonal needs and roots), for on the magic level of consciousness they were merged with the whole and expected to live on collectively after their individual sacrifice. Or they were chosen because the community could assume or ensure that they would submit and not undertake reprisal. Passive compliance seems part of the archetypal pattern. It finds expression in modern individuals notable for their loyalty and service to the family that has rejected them. They do not assert themselves and throw off the role; they identify with it masochistically, feeling profound self-hate and self-rejection. They accept their unacceptability; by carrying the shadow they serve the collective which exiles them.

Christ, a more conscious scapegoat, endured the agonies of conflict between his wish for personal survival and his acceptance of the mission he felt destined to suffer.

To resist the sacrificial role requires the capacity to hold a conscious position outside that of the ritually sustained community. Those who come into therapy have usually been driven to find such a position; they suffer a discrepancy that somewhat prevents their willing acquiescence. The individual life spirit in them has been kindled, sometimes by the very fact that they have been chosen to be the overburdened outsider, and they are beginning to suffer. Here there is some sense of carrying a role separate from individual identity. As one man realized:

> I can feel the role coming over me. I know it's not me, merely a cover, but it's what I was trained to be because that's the only way I exist—I had no other identity. Unless I acted as if things were up to me or my fault, I was invisible. I needed the attention. Now when I'm unsure of myself, it's a sure bet I'll fall back into the comfort of knowing myself the way they needed to have me, even though now I also know it's false.

Others, however, identifying only with the immolated victim, suffer from a sense of being inadequate to the task of embodying the group's necessarily pure victim. They are not able to see themselves also as the valued carriers of shadow material. Often these individuals leave therapy rather than face the loss of collective ideals (to be shadowless and pure) to which they are condemned. Unable to feel at one with the double role of pure victim and chosen sin-carrier, they accept being chosen, identified with the ideal good, and so unconsciously collude in their sacrifice.

More commonly in the scapegoat-identified individual there is a sense of being both chosen one and victim. The victim is felt as an identity with the holocausted aspect of the complex, the pre-ego. But there is also, to compensate this, a feeling of omnipotence—a sense of being the sin-carrier, dedicated to carrying guilt for necessary collective shadow qualities, thus one chosen and unusually strong. As one young woman, described by her mother to the therapist as the cause of all family problems, put it: "I was sacrificed by my mother to Jehovah because she couldn't stand up for herself. But I am stronger and I can bear it."

This suggests the curious pride and pleasure in being like Azazel's goat, the Strong One of God, able to bear so much. The individual feels affirmed in being the "rock who can hold up" and carry collective shadow material, being the Christ-like, Chosen One, selected to the task.

In automatically assuming the identity of the bad, guilty and responsible one, the individual carries more than his or her personal share in any relationship. Whatever shadow material is not consciously claimed by the other is picked up and assumed to belong to the scapegoat's burden. "Of course I have to feel everything and take away all the garbage; no one else will—or can," explained a woman who had felt responsible for maintaining harmony in her strife-ridden family. She was discussing a dream in which she made a path by clearing out hidden feces with her hands. Said another: "I was chosen to be the black one; I always absorb the dump."

One man had a dream—"I am a shiny white toilet in a public restroom. A lot of people use me"—showing that he had lost his human identity and become rigidly invulnerable and pure, in order to be able to "take all the shit" in his environment. Unusually intelligent and sensitive, he was accustomed to carrying and relieving others of shadow material. From long childhood experience as the family scapegoat, he learned to feel responsible for most problems he encountered in interpersonal relationships. It gave his affectively cold, alienated persona-ego a way of belonging to the group and being connected to those whose shadow he felt as his own. Since he perceived shadow so readily, he was valued especially by those who had little conscious self-esteem but very positive shadows, for he reflected their unconscious strengths. Others took advantage of him and vented their sadism, relieving themselves as if he were a toilet. He was, indeed, often told how "helpful" his mere presence was. Although he felt uneasy with his relationships, he confessed, "When people ask for comfort or help it means they trust me, so I get a sense of being liked."

The sense of being chosen to carry the evil and guilt of others makes it hard to separate individual responsibility from that of the collective. It makes it difficult to avoid negative inflation, and to differentiate what is one's real responsibility—that small, actual bit—from what belongs to others or to reality itself. Such discrimination is an essential task, fostered by the unconscious in dream images. One woman dreamt, "I discover that I have my own umbrella." Umbrella literally means "little shadow"—that individual burden that can protect her from whatever is falling in her environment. She had to begin to own that "little shadow," to use it rather than let herself get wet—inundated by unconscious collective material.

Another woman, after four years of therapy, was beginning to differentiate collective from personal shadow material. She dreamt: "I go to get my face scraped for blackheads. I think they are all over my face, that I am covered with them. A woman doctor says they aren't bad and only in one small cluster." The dream shows that while her identity has been based on the assumption that she is all wrong, covered with hateful black spots and "ugly" (her mother's term for being selfish or assertive), in therapy she is beginning to get another perspective. She will have to work on only a small area of her own personal shadow. Her therapeutic process forced her to grow beyond the habitual illusion of loathsomeness, introjected from the mother's self-hate. She carried it, symbiotically bonded with her mother and so often criticized that she knew no other view of herself. But she felt strong enough, as daughter, to carry the despised shadow material her mother could neither tolerate nor metabolize. She had felt her mother's message to her as: "You are strong enough to carry the shit; I need you to hate you." It was her primary experience of bonding.

Such perverted affirmation—being needed because one is inferior or hateful and loathsome—is deeply felt by many women. Women have generally carried, along with minority groups, the collective shadow of heroic Western consciousness. Such double-binding has driven many women to hysterical outbursts and to self-anaesthetizing, to righteous but abject identification with an acceptable persona, and to self-loathing. Few women do not have an active scapegoat complex. Glorified by themselves and the collective as chosen ones, and equally despised as illicit, alien, second-class and victim, they are too often the silent and patient vessels of necessary, but derogated, shadow qualities.

Problems of Self-Assertion

Assertiveness, seen as aggression, has been culturally repressed into the Christian shadow. Scapegoat-identified individuals have learned to fear assertion. They have been taught that it is bad, and have often been severely punished for expressing it. They tend to deny their self-protective instinct to refuse abuse, in order that they may better accept the role chosen for them.

Parental envy of the chosen child's strength, and the cruel idealization that wants the child to be a perfect figure to satisfy the scapegoater's magical standards, provide an illusion of control and security in a difficult world. Both of these powerful projections destroy the scapegoated child's relation to its assertive and dependency instincts. The child feels a multiple bind. Seen by the scapegoating parent as too powerful because identified with the feared shadow, the child develops personae precociously to cover and mediate these projections. On the other hand, the child cannot achieve the ideals of the accuser and feels worthless and endlessly guilty. Realistic rage and need are split. Others may sense the unmediated, hidden rage and demandingness or feel manipulated or double-bound by the scapegoat victim-ego's fragility and the alienated persona-ego's guilt. But the individual suffering the scapegoat complex cannot initially bear confrontation. The complex has become a personal identity. Assertion and need are merely sources of more helplessness and guilt, feeding into self-hate.

The assertive instinct, as a body-based defense of integrity, is radically distorted as it operates within the scapegoat-identified adult. It is often so denied or split it cannot come to consciousness. As a result, there are only sadistic or artificial controls, not conscious, disciplined aggression. One man described how he experienced this wound to the instinct:

> I never thought when I didn't like something it might mean it wasn't right for me. Saying no was bad. And not wanting felt like my fault. The negative feeling meant something was wrong with me—not a way to be in touch with an interior truth. Like if I was given a bad mushroom, I ought to eat it and not be negative. To refuse what I hated was impossible so I ate even what was bad for me and turned all my No's into blame and self-hate. My instinctive reactions must be off, way off now. In fact, I don't know what they might be.

As a child he had been forced to eat food to which he was allergic and seen merely as ungrateful and spoiled when he tried to reject it. He still suffered the violation of his inner system's integrity in mistrust of his instinctive assertive and self-protective emotions and behaviors. He bound them with artificial ideals and with guilt.

Scapegoat-identified individuals as children often experienced unmediated aggression in the tyrannical unconscious outbursts of the parental shadow. As the witness and/or focus of such behavior, they know it feels awesome, even annihilating. They often have no experience of parentally metabolized aggression to permit them to distinguish between power as an ego necessity and its misuse in crushing, punitive-feeling destructiveness. Thus they fear to wield it at all unless and until it is "all cleaned up." One man expressed this, "I put Chlorox on my angry emotions." This ego-maiming need to purify and denature assertiveness until it is expressed only in passive-aggressive modes, is regularly imaged in dreams; for example:

> I hide my Women's Lib button in the washing machine.

> I keep trying to wipe up the table so I can work. It's never clean enough to put my papers down, so I keep wiping.

When it is directly expressed, aggression usually takes the form of impulsive outbursts against the therapist or others. The individual here identifies with the condemning Azazel scapegoater, in righteous accusations against others, themselves, the therapist or the general follies of the world. Here the power drive functions with the sanction of collective mores, and expressing it thus may provide moments of relief from the loneliness of feeling outcast. In one case a young man was temporarily relieved of his own sense of guilt and rejection when he found a younger sibling incurring parental exile similar to his own experience. He poured forth an outburst of vindictiveness and blame against the sibling and then felt suddenly close to his parents, almost accepted, and momentarily vindicated.

Generally, however, such expressions of accusatory power erupt unconsciously in outbursts of rage that just "happen" to the individual, leaving a residue of remorse and guilty relief but no inkling of personal responsibility for the outburst. There is also a tendency to stockpile a whole series of annoyances until the pressure of the affect can burst through with an exciting rush that overwhelms the superego's prohibitions. These rushes can even become addictive "adrenaline-highs," a form of an altered state of consciousness. Then integration of the affect is resisted, for without the rush there is no relief from tension. It also holds the illusion of the ecstasy of primary or "uroboric" bliss, which the scapegoated individual longs for from across the wilderness of despair.[53]

Often aggression erupts, rationalized with righteous indignation, against "fascists," or "bad social conditions," with a compulsive need to have something done to change the outer balance of power. Here the accuser is felt as the redeemer. This permits expression of the affect. But this expression depends on the automatic assumption of the accuser that outer and inner reality are split into good and bad; a good to be forced into being, and a bad to be combatted. The complex enforces such adversarial polarizations because on the level of magic consciousness there is no alternative to such simplistic either/or splitting. Ambivalence is impossible without an ego. But for the scapegoat-identified individual, such splitting aids in the expression of otherwise reprehensible assertion. And while culturally it serves to release aggression safely against a perceived enemy, it also encourages shadow projections. As one woman finally verbalizing her rebelliousness against her parents and the mores of her home town put it:

> If I'm not defiant and brand them as evil, then I have to brand me as wicked, because I'm not like them, and they always made me feel that. But somebody has to be bad to justify anger.

Unless the condemning Azazel is identified with through such collective grandiose and impulsive thrusts against those onto whom the shadow is projected, direct power cannot easily be claimed by scapegoat-identified individuals at all.[54] As part of the collective shadow, aggressive impulses are seen as a cause of rejection. Those identified with the complex keep such "sick" and "evil" impulses hidden in an effort to avert further rejection. Theodor Gaster writes of the suffering servant or *pharmakon*,

> as one from whom men hide their face . . . [for] the Servant is a sick man, and in ancient and primitive thought, sickness implies possession by a demon . . . "smitten of God (i.e., demon-struck) and afflicted (i.e., plagued)." Now such demonic influences can be relayed to others by a mere glance. . . . The person who is demonically possessed had to keep his face covered, lest he pass the evil to others . . . sometimes, too, the necessary disguise is effected by whitewash.[55]

In the modern scapegoat-identified individual, the need to keep hidden what is branded as evil prevents its deintegration from the archaic Self and causes certain typical distortions in the power drive. With the often unconscious rebellion and resentment of the martyred victim, and the fear of accepting or releasing such culturally proscribed qualities, goes the persona of innocence, virtue and competence—a mask that might fool the judging accuser. Thus assertion is veiled behind what is aptly called a false-self system, since the veiling leaves a sense of unease and falsity.

Veiling also leads to a series of passive-aggressive distortions— manoeuvres which permit some expression of the split-off impulses, but expression that is indirect and usually unconscious. Among these there is baiting; there is cold vengeance and magic vengeance (both deriving from the primitive *lex talionis,* an eye for an eye, a tooth for a tooth); there is innocent hostility; there is spite against the Self; there is magic suppression. And there are enslavement to the accuser, self-immolation and generalized, fatalistic doom.

I use this spectrum of behaviors as a rough diagnostic tool, for it provides a guide to the kind and degree of access to assertiveness that the individual has. Generally, individuals with their predominant modes in the latter categories have their aggressive impulses not only split off but also turned against their own victim-ego self-destructively, for their identity is totally dependent on placating the accusing scapegoater. With these persons, therapeutic work must proceed very cautiously. Those operating in the former categories tend to have more ego strength, to be increasingly willing to acknowledge their rage in the safe, therapeutic container, and may even enjoy the feelings involved in the impulse's release and control. They may call their enjoyment "vile pleasure," as one man did, but it moves them toward integrating the assertive, competitive and triumphant feelings that so badly need to be actively related to consciousness.

The first modality, which I call baiting, involves a safely veiled expression of the individual's own anger. This subtly prods the other into an outburst. Sometimes the baiting is at least partially conscious. One young woman expressed this:

> To be in control of emotion is strong and superior. When the other person goes berserk, I watch and secretly gloat. It's a tactic of being a bitch. I'm deliberately vicious, but so cold-bloodedly and virtuously, it makes the other person strangle himself. No one knows I'm full of hatred myself.

This woman had moved along the spectrum from a predominant mode of self-immolation and was beginning to enjoy her assertiveness.

At other times the baiting is unconscious, in which case the aggression is felt by the therapist and others as projected affect. When this is reacted to defensively it often serves to legitimize the scapegoat-identified individual's anger. Such justification may then permit more direct expression of the emotion, which the judgmental inner scapegoater otherwise condemns. Aggressive action in the service of a cause, which directs the individual's need for assertion safely toward the collective's scapegoat or enemy, and aggressive action in self-defense, are prime modes of such justifiable release. Baiting the other to attack first sometimes—when the instinct is not too broken—gives the scapegoat seeming permission to defend oneself. The anger is then masked as valid self-defense. This serves to coalesce the victim-ego, for the expressed anger often carries the fury of vengeance against a hurtful figure in the individual's past whose identity is projected onto the person being baited.[56] But it can also become a mere discharge, acting out a repetitive compulsion that cannot be satisfied until its roots are interpreted.

Another form of assertion is the cold vengeance that operates out of the usually unconscious scapegoater part of the complex. It is perceived through the chill it throws over the relationship when the proudly denied need is not met, or when hurt and anger are experienced but denied expression. This can abruptly end a liaison, "axing" the offending party and condemning the other to exile. At one point with a patient a coldness fell into the sessions. Only later did we realize it was because I had not sent him a postcard over my vacation. The request had never been made that I do so, but it operated on a magic level, as a rule I was expected to know, and I was punished for having betrayed what he considered was his trust. He had a clear, albeit unexpressed and conditional, moral code: if he was good, he would be rewarded with whatever he needed, if I was a good therapist-parent. By failing to comply, either I had judged him as not good and withheld affection as punishment, or I had failed in my role. Either way, he felt I had betrayed him and so must be rejected in turn, but secretly, in order to protect himself from my retaliation. When all this became conscious, we could appreciate the longing for an adequately caring relationship that lay buried beneath the cold vengeance.

One woman, at a point in therapy when she began to experience the long repressed, unwanted pain of her childhood deprivation and her unfilled dependency needs, had the following dream:

> I am in a bus that has no wheels and doesn't go on tracks. It rides above the panorama. The driver took over the bus on some kind of a mission. He is all-powerful over the rest of us, and shows that anything can be done by driving past various cities. He has a goal

in an old-fashioned, arctic town. He backs down a narrow street and finds the man he sought. The goal is vengeance.

Work on the dream led this woman to see the powerful animus which kept her way of going through life in the collective mode, off the ground, driven by a sense of retribution for old hurts. It brought up her vengeful rejection of her father because he had left the family, hurting her deeply and making her feel weak and needy. And it showed how the same attitude threatened to close off her affects and the therapeutic relationship because it was exposing the old wounds, going into the cold, arctic territory of repression to settle old accounts.[57]

The mask that covers the victim's helpless rage, and the ensuing fear and hatred of the collectivity ruled by the sadistic accuser, combine to create a kind of innocent hostility, a subtle thwarting. One woman, whom I had asked to draw a dream image, sweetly handed me back the white paper on which she had drawn doodles in invisible white crayon. She was too afraid even to feel, much less express her own "No" except veiled in compliance. Her anger was triggered by an expectation she felt was unfair, but which she could not refuse for fear of being rejected.

Another form of such innocent hostility involves the "throwing of guilt"—assuming an attitude of such pain that the other is expected to feel sorry for the sufferer and to make restitution for "what you did to me." This mode calls upon an habitual, tacit propriety, which avoids the necessity for direct expression of feelings because both parties are expected to obey the same collective laws. A woman explained this:

> I'll be nice to you to make sure you'll be nice to me. If you're not, I'll feel self-righteous and angry. The only controls are social ones we both agree to. I depend on making you agree because I don't trust my instinct or experience. We both just have to be obedient and collude together to obey the social rules. The rules my mother taught me. I don't call you names or tell you if I'm mad because I can't function if I'm aggressive, I feel so guilty. Even as a child I remember feeling so guilty I had to confess if I was bad. So I have to make you feel guilty if you hurt me.

In such cases direct expression of the person's hurt or anger is inhibited by the collective's introjected rules, now part of the accuser part of the complex. They can merely be insinuated, so the shared law—"thou shalt not hurt"—strikes the aggressor from within, without the victim's having to take active measures on his or her own behalf. When this does not work in therapy, the inner conflict becomes manifest. Sometimes, when the therapist merely affirms and restates the complaints and does not provide the recompensing concrete action (an apology, for instance), the victim can be finally roused to such overt fury as to become able to see the angry demandingness under the guise of "poor-me." But sometimes such affirmation gets co-opted by the inner accuser and the victim regresses to self-hate and guilt for complaining.

Underlying all of these veiled assertion manoeuvres is an apotropaic intent to ward off anticipated punishment. As one young woman expressed this:

> If I punish myself first, others won't do it to me—like getting there ahead of the pack or playing dead so the attackers leave me alone. All I have to do is something mean to myself and then let the other person care for me.

In scapegoat-identified individuals who are unable to acknowledge even this degree of anger, retaliation operates in secret and on a magic level. One young man, upset by what he felt was callousness, "atomized" the offenders in fantasy and could then ignore them as well as his own hurt sensitivities. He became aware of what he was doing through a dream image:

> I am in a supermarket. Near the checkout are shelves full of voodoo dolls. I want the tiny one that is like a shrunken woman. The checkout woman gives a lecture on not buying any of the dolls. She is like my mother.

Here the voodoo fetish stands for magic retaliation, for the man was too fearful to express any direct animosity. He felt unable to accept his intense grandiose-archaic hatred for both the imperfectly-giving therapist and his rejecting-demanding mother, "because the gods punish mother-haters, like Orestes." His own rage terrified him; he said he was tempted to terminate the analysis rather than confront the therapist with his rage and disappointment for her "callousness." He also felt unable to accept responsibility for "hurting a woman" and incurring more rejection, so he would reject her "first and finally." Previously he had bound and shrunk his hate with reaction formations—caretaking his drunken mother and now trying to caretake his therapist—rather than express his negative transference so as to find its human dimensions.

A woman who had experienced tales of her mother's attempts to abort her and who felt herself keenly to be the family black sheep dreamt of a voodoo fetish of herself: "A cold, judgmental man is sticking pins into my legs. It hurts. I am a voodoo doll of myself." Here the spiteful mode of masochistic assertion against oneself is revealed. The animus painfully destroys the woman's own feeling standpoint when she identifies with the mode of magic vengeance, allowing the animus to turn her power drive against herself. She had felt misinterpreted by the analyst in the previous session and would never have expressed it openly but for the dream. The next night she dreamt: "I fill my shoes with water to spite my mother. It ruins them." Of "spite" she said, "I ruin my life to make mother feel guilty, to make her pay." Yet she was surprised to have the aggression of this remark pointed out to her, for she could only conceive of herself as "nice" and "innocent"—not hurtful. She believed that as long as she was only harmful to herself she was still "nice"—acceptable to others and to her own superego.

This spiteful mode operates according to the infantile principle: "It serves you right when you hurt me."[58] Or as an old German proverb puts it: "My mother won't give me gloves to wear; it serves her right if my hands freeze."

There are two roots to this distorted and sometimes suicidal manifestation of the power drive. The first is the lack of separation between the victim-ego and the scapegoater. They are symbiotically fused at the magic level of consciousness. Because of the overpowering negativity of the scapegoater, individual consciousness has not deintegrated out of the level of the body-Self. Thus any assertion against the authority of the demonic Azazel or the outer parental figure involves also hurting the victim-ego and the unvalued body. The unworthy "me" is still the unworthy body to be gotten rid of. "I will starve myself, become a slit, and then I'll be rid of the sense of being abnormal," one anorexic woman asserted. This same woman fantasized cutting off her right forefinger as a commitment to a new life, free of rigidly controlling imperatives and accusations, as a way of getting rid of the "terrible finger of god." (Recall that Orestes cut off his finger in an attempt to appease the guilt-inducing Erinyes.) It is an attitude that goes along with a deeply embedded sense of worthlessness. As this same woman said, "I am an outcast: to hell with me."

With such individuals, who mix self-destruction and spiteful assertion and who have lost the instinct for self-defense, it is vitally important early in therapy to try to objectify the sadistic accuser as a Thou which can be symbolically confronted by both therapist and patient in an alliance against its effects. Otherwise assertion may take the form of impulsive self-punitive acts, the result of the sadism turned against the body. But such acts may also be the result of the beginnings of assertion against Azazel while yet insufficiently dis-identified from him.

The second root of the self-punitive assertion is habitual and originally life-preserving, for spitefulness is the way the child survived. Aggression is turned against both the rejector and the person's own needs and wounds. But behind the clenched teeth of defiance is an urge to live. Spite hides the hurts of alienation and the lack of someone to meet dependency needs. For the child its use meant that a core of integrity could survive. Self-spite and self-accusation guarded this core from a scrutiny which was felt to be destructive. The child could both hide a precious value and refuse to be fed emotionally in order not to take in reactions and responses too painful and poisonous to bear.

For instance, the above-mentioned anorexic woman's first memory was of her father's punishing her by hanging the lollipop she had wanted before lunch just out of reach in her crib: the fate of Tantalus. Her only defense had been to side with the punisher-father, to reject her desire for the sweets of life. She came proudly to manifest her integrity by denying her need for tenderness and feeling herself above such crass things. She explained that she thus showed superior strength and self-discipline through her contempt for the "indulgences" her parents enjoyed. Much of one phase of therapy involved her using her energy to get what she had to relearn to desire. She had been told that "what you get is not what you want, it's what Santa Claus gives you, so be grateful for whatever you get." Desire itself had become a torture, hence she repressed her desires. The repression and denial gave her a sense of power and comfort; but it also set need and power at odds with each other (a persistent pattern that often lies at the root of eating disorders). The conflict also operated in the transference, for example when she would ask for suggestions only to find herself rejecting them. This fueled her panic and increased her neediness. Nurturance was tantalizingly close but had to be rejected because it might still involve enslavement to the punitive giver.

Enslavement to Azazel in an attempt to win his favor involves another form of self-punishment. Here aggression is in the hands of the accuser, and the individual colludes with Azazel. This form of assertion is without the ego strength of defiance. It seems to go with a sense of self-immolation which is harder to work with in therapy. It may only be apparent in bouts of self-denigration or irrelevant idealistic talk, triggered by a flicker of anger that is immediately fused masochistically with the condemnations of the accuser.

Dreams often illustrate the degree of willing enslavement. One young woman dreamt: "At a party I dance only with a dark man, like Mr. X. I try to please him, put on make-up that makes me feel foolish." To Mr. X., she associated a man who was dead, but who had tormented his children with perfectionistic standards and driven one son to suicide. In the dream it is a dance of death for her, but she so longs for acceptance that she is drawn to connect to the very one who would destroy her; she makes herself up to be doll-like and agreeable, a persona that may fool others but makes ludicrous her own life's individual dance.

At another time she dreamt:

> I am in a shed working for my boss. I have to go out and get children four years old. I bring them back in couples, a girl and a boy, and stack them up on top of each other so he can kill them. I don't like it, but I have to; he's my boss.

Here her creativity and independence, which she associated to the children and to herself in nursery school, are brutally disposed of by the sadistic animus boss. In her external life situation she was compulsively overworking to exhaustion, trying to earn the favor of a man she felt to be totally irresponsible; but she fantasized being needed, valued and rewarded by him, and could not, therefore, give up the enslavement. She sought omnipotently to redeem him, as she had tried to redeem her father. Much later in therapy, after a positive transference had developed, she dreamt of her weak, placatory but judgmental mother as a Bolshevik. With that image she began to feel there was a possibility of finding feminine strength and a purposeful, even ruthless, manner of standing her own ground. She moved from suicidal depression to cold vengeance against oppression. Until then she had lacked experience of any mode of self-affirmation other than collusion with the aggressive self-hate.

Closely related to this woman's earlier attitude is the apathetic siding with the accuser of the victim-ego. This leads to a generalized sense of doom. Here the alienated victim-ego is brittle and only minimally developed, and there is little capacity to function at all.

One despairs of there being anything except pathology and evil in oneself, and anything but misery and aggression in the outer and inner environments. There is little purpose in living, and typically such individuals expect or plan to die young. They assume any action is doomed to failure and so give up, with a sense of futility and "why bother," before they start. Usually they have not found a viable way to hold or to avoid their early pain and still associate it with abject, victimized helplessness and intense rejection. In such cases there is a real danger that repressed volcanic rage, breaking the fragile shell of the poorly developed persona-ego, will lead to psychosis.

When assertion is held so totally by the demonic accuser, as it is in these last two modalities, the therapist may need to lend his or her own strength to the patient to drive the demon from its victim. Silent, intense visualization of this action in therapy sessions can be very effective, but the result may not last long since the energies that spoil life are those served as powerful by the victim-ego. Such persons may need daily contact with the therapist, or at least a supportive therapeutic environment in order to build a trusted relationship and to learn behaviors with which to cope—just to feel even minimally effective. At such times and during the therapeutic regression, the use of transition objects and ceremonies can be potent supports through the scapegoat-identified person's therapeutic return to the despair and abandonment-depression of the wilderness.[59]

In all cases involving the spectrum of passive-aggressive manoeuvres, one of the major tasks of therapy is to confirm assertion as acceptable, necessary and valid. The therapist must first help to make these behaviors conscious, and then affirm them by standing against the undifferentiated demonic prohibitions which forbid all direct assertion. The therapist must also be willing to help find viable modes of releasing the transpersonal instinct of self-assertion, both within the therapeutic container and outside it. This means being willing to focus on, elicit and endure expressions of anger when they occur, for almost all of the above manoeuvres will be played out in the regressive phases of the transference-countertransference situation. Learning to release and control assertion directly in the safe, therapeutic container is an essential step on the way to relating consciously to one's own individuality.

Ultimately, at the more active end of the assertion spectrum, the accuser's vengeful *lex talionis* begins to operate in the form of the primitive assumption that "if I suffer, others should too." At some point in therapy this initially vindictive and enviously destructive statement needs to be seriously considered. It then can become a conscious questioning of the collective morality which the scapegoat accepted and which was originally responsible for the feeling of exile. Here, in a typical angry outburst, self-assertion comes forth as blaming vengeance and hatred:

> It's not my burden only, so why don't others have to carry their share? It felt forced on me, why not on them? It's their game and I can't play it. I only feel worthless. But why do I even have to? Let them suffer for a change.

Such emotions need full acceptance, for they mark the beginning of disidentification from the alienated and victim aspects of the complex and the beginning of conscious, individual assertion, albeit in the mode of the accusing scapegoater. In the long run these emotions bring forth questions of justice and responsibility and of individual calling—"Why me?" and "What is my way apart from that of the collective?"—questions which ask not merely, "What have I done wrong?" but also turn to reflect on the meaning of the ego's suffering in the larger context of conscience and the Self. Such questions open up into problems of transpersonal destiny and of individualized responsibility and integrity. As Jung puts this:

> No matter how much parents and grandparents may have sinned against the child, the man who is really adult will accept these sins as his own condition which has to be reckoned with. Only a fool is interested in other people's guilt, since he cannot alter it. The wise man learns only from his own guilt. He will ask himself: Who am I that all this should happen to me? To find the answer to this fateful question he will look into his own heart.[60]

But before the scapegoat-identified individual can ask this question of his or her heart, she or he will have to look at the anguish and anger there and learn from them how to grow beyond the symptoms of guilt-bearing and martyred self-rejection that are major components of the negatively inflated identity. Then—and only after claiming the power to act aggressively and assertively within the collective for one's individual needs—can true submission to individual vocation and fate begin to take place. Premature renunciation of assertion maintains the instinctual energy in the wilderness, split off from consciousness. It does not foster disidentification from the scapegoat complex, but merely colludes with the accuser.

Need Satisfaction

In the scapegoat complex desirousness too is spoiled, devalued and repressed. Often it remains split off from consciousness, hiding within the hidden victim-ego's yearning for acceptance. The demonic superego, like a punitive, Victorian Yahweh, stands against the pleasures of the flesh, against the gratification of needs, including dependency. It brands them as selfish, weak, shameful or greedy indulgences which cannot be admitted. The alienated ego acquiesces in the punitive deprivation with a sense of stoic pride, hiding the victim-ego's split-off neediness and dependency. The individual identified with the scapegoat must carry the repressed shadow impulses, but their manifestation can only be secret and projected or unconscious and impulsive. Inadvertent, personal need gratification is disavowed with: "I hate myself for that," "It wasn't my fault, I was coerced into it," or discounted as "not fun any-way"—all attempts to placate Azazel and to avoid the guilt of evading his automatic prohibition.

This poses a problem for the therapist who serves as the voice of reality and warns against the consequences of impulsivity. For the therapist can then immediately become identified with the accusing Azazel, while the patient polarizes into helpless, guilty victim, unable to differentiate part from whole—identified totally with the piece of shadow behavior on the magic level of *pars pro toto*. Elaborate appeasement rituals may be set up. When one woman began her sessions with protestations, "I'm so sorry, I know you'll hate this . . .," it was clear that the therapist was seen as the scapegoater to be placated. More dangerous is the problem of evasion and silence, when one anticipates negative judgments and simply withholds information about guilt-incurring material. Naming the reality, even mildly, is at this point counterproductive. More useful is interpreting the impasse, both by expressing appreciation in order to validate the person's need and by caringly reflecting on the potential harm of impulsivity. This gives the patient a feeling of alliance and renders powerless the painful alienation and polarization of the complex's basic structure.

Since open assertion in the service of personal need is initially impossible, and often (as discussed above) power functions against need, identification with the complex necessitates behaviors which might be called inhibited gratifications. A few of these behaviors are disguised request and negated request, magic demandingness, gratification with self-punishment, and anesthesia of needs. In all of them behavior in accord with the accuser's prohibition veils and distorts open expression of the split-off impulse. A particular form of need gratification characteristic of the scapegoat complex is compulsive caretaking of others—a satisfaction of the instinct in projection.

Disguised request functions to veil the individual's own neediness and dependency with a collectively sanctioned behavior. Sometimes the demand is for socially acceptable help for others or a cause. Here the individual is gratified both by feeling the "good helper" and by identifying with the receivers of bounty. Sometimes the need is disguised as a socially legitimate debt. "I've been coming to therapy, you owe me that," one woman expressed it. The giving of gifts may be a form of this disguised request, especially when there is a hidden demand for recompense to balance the exchange or when they serve as a defense to ward off expressions of anger or need. Sometimes the individual asks for need satisfaction under the guise of caring for the caretaker. One young man asked me if I was cold when he wanted the window closed. His inner accuser told him he would be weak to express need if he alone felt discomfort. On another level, he implied that I was emotionally cold to his unexpressed need, but he was not sure enough of this to risk a direct request.

Negated request is a mixture of discouragement, hostility and need: "I know you won't give it to me," said one man, "but I'll ask anyway." Usually the expression is less overt; the individual assumes rejection before the fact and only conveys anger or veils the fear of rejection by rejecting first. One young woman, who tried several times abruptly to leave therapy, hid what she viewed as her shameful dependency on the therapist by her rejection of the whole process. She was so identified with her stoic, proud, alienated ego that she felt either rejection or validation of her neediness would be too painful to bear.

Magic demandingness is seen in the patient's need to have the therapist supply gratification without any overt action on the patient's part. One cannot express a specific desire because the issue is globalized and assumes the inevitability of total rejection. One woman expressed this: "I can only ask for something if I am sure I'll get it. To have you say no seems like a total rejection of me. All of me is in every request." Her addiction to rejection was so strong that she assumed and expected it.

On the magic level, where part can stand for whole, one identifies and rejects oneself with each request. Here overt request seems to endanger the asker. Instead, the individual safely and passively fantasizes gratification or assumes the therapist will intuit one's needs and "be sensitive enough to supply them," like the good mother of an infant. "It's okay if I receive without asking; that's like a grace. Otherwise I have to do everything on my own, even if I can't, and it's lonely." So sensitive are scapegoat-identified individuals to nuances implying rejection that they can feel very deeply hurt when the therapist does not understand subtle needs—for silence, empathy, "the right word at the right moment," etc. It may not be enough to interpret each symbiotic, magic demand, for that often feels punitive or critical. Therapeutic empathy, sensitively mirroring the needs of the preverbal victim-ego, is called for. Only then can the dependency feel validated enough for these individuals to begin to build some trust in their own worthiness to receive. They begin to feel they are not just garbage or pariahs.

There are deep wounds in the area of need satisfaction when this mode or the following ones operate. Such severe inhibition in the capacity to validate need was explained by two scapegoat-identified patients:

> If I had to ask my mother, it meant I accused her of being stingy, and I felt too guilty.

> If I asked anything, my mother made me feel it was painful to her, even dangerous. She was sick and I just burdened her worse. My needs are dangerous, maybe murderous. She did die.

The introjected stingy or punitive parent instills fear of one's own seemingly bad and devouring, even murderous, desirousness. This is compensated by an inflated sense of the power of the affect. For when all need is repressed, it remains archaically fused with the grandiose Self and no discrimination can be made between valid and excessive dependency. The individual fears to be "as demanding as a greedy infant or a mugger."

Gratification with self-punishment is exemplified in the secret eating binge. In several cases bulimic women were overcome with a desire to consume large amounts of non-diet food when no watchful eye was present to prevent this concrete and primal mode of self-nurture. But they ate so fast they could not taste the illicit pleasure, and for several days afterward they punished themselves by fasting and self-hatred. Two bulimic women brought dreams with the motif of a diabetic in connection with their ravenous and punished binge. One woman explained her eating problem symbolically through the image of diabetes:

> Diabetes is an incapacity to assimilate sweetness [of life] and requires a dose of insulin. You have to be careful what you eat and also careful of the medicine that controls it or you can go into shock. The balance is off. My balance is off because I can't really feel either need or fullness. They are both frightening; and they are both there all the time. That must be impossible.

Another bulimic woman dreamt of a hungry child whom she took out and fed occasionally, then returned to its dark cupboard.

At the extreme end of the spectrum of repression is anaesthesia of needs. In such cases one identifies with the accuser's demonic imperatives against need satisfaction, and dissociates to prevent body messages from reaching consciousness. Hunger, thirst, the need to excrete, pain itself, as well as the emotional needs for attention, time and other caretaking, are so habitually denied that they are not noticed. This gives an illusion of proud self-sufficiency that covers the pain and shame of never having received sufficient care. It is analogous to emotional anorexia.

One woman covered her misery with the virtue of stoicism. "I won't get, so I'll go it alone, not need. It's better to be a hermit." She recalled a childhood fascination with the Mandan sun dancers and described how she had learned to discipline herself to not feel bodily and psychological tortures. She wore a mask of untouchable independence that had preserved her. But when her anaesthesia began to dissipate, opening its defensive portals at first for moments, then longer, she felt an excruciating sense of the uncompanioned, multiple agonies and deprivations that had been dormant and walled off. As they began to enter consciousness, they ruptured her identification with the alienated persona and caused her to fall into the "numb chaos of unknown territory." Thus, she returned in this process to the underworld or wilderness, but now companioned by the therapist. This time she could tell and experience her grief, dependency and rage, and learn to endure these aspects of her own vitality.

Since the scapegoat-identified individual tends to be the victim of split-off and unconscious impulses as well as of the negative judgments against the expression of impulse, the helpless-me can do quite unspeakable, even sociopathic things, from stealing what is desired—overtly or by manipulation—to becoming entangled in vampire-like liaisons. So long repressed, the passions stay concrete; what is desired is leapt at or drifted into. Responsibility, in terms of the authority to be conscious of impulses or the authority to control them, is held by so negative an accusing and perfectionistic demon that there is often no alternative to the cycle of all-or-nothing impulsivity and guilt—a psychological analogue to bulimia.

A common result of the hidden and projected dependency may be a growing fear coupled with secret rage and resentment. One feels taken advantage of by others. While this may be true, and even the result of the scapegoat's excessive caretaking, it may be also a perseverative reaction from the misuse of one's capacities by those closest in childhood. Or it may indicate some projected and secret wish to take advantage of another in order to gratify dependency needs. Sometimes this only comes to awareness in analysis when the therapist is thought to be stealing one's perceptual gifts or dream material, or even the fee.

Initially in scapegoat-identified individuals, dependency—and hence demandingness—is split off. The repressed demandingness— "I want what I want," in primitive, arrogant, greedy form—functions as a hidden assumption that the world owes the scapegoat recompense for service as the overburdened, suffering victim of the collective. This demand for justice lies hidden as a compensation behind the complex. Balancing the scapegoat is a repressed prince or princess, one chosen to be served by others, given the goodness of life and protected from evil. This can be seen in fantasies of power, satisfaction and redemption. Like the passive, unredeemed victim of myth and fairytales—Andromeda chained, Sleeping Beauty, Snow White in her casket—there is evoked an image of one who simply awaits rescue and leaves all assertion to others.

In the early stages of therapeutic work this may manifest as a childlike demand that the therapist take over ego functions for the patient. "You have to do it for me," threatened one young man, "otherwise I'll have to kill myself." He was confronted with the need to find a job to support himself and realized he was unable even to use the telephone. On the one hand he felt too special and potentially important to do ordinary work and was afraid to confront his limits in reality. But also he feared to undertake any training program, feeling so inadequate to the simplest tasks. His sense of coherent identity was weakened by identification with both prince and pauper. He suffered a genuine incapacity, and the therapist had to honor his need by serving as a model of ego functioning in the manner of a caring parent. This entailed teaching skills by role playing. He and the therapist took different roles to enact the phone calls he feared, and finally he made an initial call during a session.

At other times such dependency needs may entail concrete as well as symbolic fulfillment; although sometimes patients may express a desire for food or a hug and be far from able to receive such care in reality. Then it is necessary to first work through the defenses against such desire.

Later in therapy, the young man mentioned above began to argue, "I won't take care of myself. I want someone else to do it for me." Such stubbornness is already an advance, revealing a flowing of libido and a nascent capacity to demand assertively. The process can get stuck here for a long time while the individual tests this new-found potency and the tolerance of the therapist onto whom is projected the accepting Self.

At a still later stage in the work with this same patient, his demandingness had a different context, as a dream illustrated: "I am being driven by my brother. He stops to get the car serviced, and he pretends to be the head of the company so he can get free service. I don't say anything." To the driver the dreamer associated a man who feels he ought to get what he wants and who asks a lot of others. Here that shadow attitude drives; it is an unconscious assumption. It tries to cheat to avoid the responsibility of paying for needs to be met. It is inflated, pretending to be "the head of the company," one to whom free service is due. The dream-ego stays uninvolved, a passive onlooker, but the effect of the dream was to prod the dreamer into taking on the responsibility of which he was now capable.

In the process of healing, the ego must become active and responsible, even heroic, in pursuit of its needs. Ultimately, the repressed regal demandingness of the scapegoat complex becomes the royal core of the ego, the center which can act with authority, initiative and responsibility, thus permitting freedom from the accusing Azazel's reign. For this reason, when demandingness appears overtly in therapy with severely scapegoat-identified patients, it is to be welcomed and not automatically frustrated.[62] It is a positive sign that the grip of the demonic, depriving negativity is being loosened by instinctual hungers. These break up the old gestalt of the complex and enable corrective therapeutic experiences, which in turn permit the hidden victim-ego to enter life and to develop.

Their appearance means there is already some trust that needs can be met, that the world is not merely frustratingly rule-bound and malevolent. Taming these needs and affects with acceptance, discipline and humor is a long, trying process. In individuals identified with the scapegoat, humor and playfulness are generally superficial covers of the alienated persona or entirely lacking. These need to be fostered in order to provide a counterpart to the usually heavy, tragic view of life, and to permit serious creative expression.

The demands of the pre-ego, the hidden Self-child, need to be patiently supported and endured by the therapist until the patient's process suggests that the time has arrived for self-discipline of the unleashed greed or rage. In one case of a persistently demanding woman, who evaded and resisted all limit setting as if she were testing her worth, the image of an army officer finally appeared in a dream. Work on this image enabled her to recognize the positive value of discipline and courage in the face of adversity. Until that time, she had not been able to discriminate between genuine need and arrogant greed, for the scapegoating inner accuser had confused the two in her experience even more than her parents had done. The therapist's calling attention to her greediness—which the woman herself imaged as "a very demanding little girl" and "a tyrant child"—or trying to limit the excessive, daily demands for time and attention, evoked only overwhelming rage which upset her so severely that she tried to deny all dependency.

This woman's mature, adaptive mind, as a partner in the therapeutic alliance, agreed that her demands needed limits, but she had learned to associate discipline with punishment and shame. The preferences of both analyst and analysand were thwarted by the autonomous psyche which enforced its slow, organic process. In the course of this process the woman's relation to her instinct moved from the concretistic, magic level to some capacity for symbolic realization and expression; from the mistrust which fueled her stealing of the analyst's time, to the capacity to hold a constant image of a trusted source of gratification. Only then could she find satisfaction in imaginary sustenance while she waited for its appropriate, concrete appearance. The rampant desirousness marked the initial stage of a process known in alchemy as *coagulatio* (solidification or concretization).[63] It brought into life the beginnings of a new image of the Self as beneficent and accepting, capable of being trusted to respond with generous relatedness as well as with helpful, adaptive discipline. This in turn provided a model for a motivated ego able to find its own balance between regal claiming and regal, related generosity—healing her old split between masochistic self-sacrifice and arrogant, impulsive demandingness.

The gratification of even small desires for scapegoat-identified individuals may initially be so potent, however, that it may seem dangerously intoxicating. Emily Dickinson expressed this when she wrote, "One drop of joy and I tip drunken . . ." Indeed, the somatic symptom of dizziness may accompany the experience of non-judgmental acceptance and concern. Gratification also may evoke an overwhelming gratitude that seems to threaten the victim-ego with an indebtedness comparable to enslavement to the new source of nourishment. The fear of this enslavement caused one man to fall back into argumentativeness and blaming each time he experienced acceptance. By retreating to black and white categorization under the accuser, he sought to stave off inundation by the unconscious.

This means that doses of experience which run counter to the expectations of the complex must be small enough to be assimilated. A man who was particularly sensitive to the overwhelming power of positive and caring experiences brought in dreams with images of "snail mills" or minutely calibrated allergy shots. The alternative was an image of the sudden thaw that threatened to flood his house every time he felt that the therapist "gave the gift of understanding" to his loneliness, anger or need. It was hard for him to see that such positive experiences come ultimately from the Self, for he could not relate symbolically to emotion. His alienated persona-ego used intellectual skills defensively. His victim-ego was still on the magic level and literalistic. Neither could connect affect with image. The therapist thus became like the parents who had rejected him and whose acceptance he craved with a devouring that he projected onto the therapist. Gratification and being devoured became intertwined, for he feared that the whole force of the unconscious would come through every experience that was not held off by identification with the doomed, burdened, strong victim. He could not take more than a few months of therapy at a time, and felt safer when he could see the therapist as incompetent or in the role of accuser. The positive transference was for many years an agonizing threat to him.

6

The Scapegoat—Messiah Image

It is significant that the two archetypal patterns, that of the sacrificed one who is also a suffering, despised and rejected servant, and that of the ruler, come together in the Messiah image. For individuals identified with the scapegoat archetype, this image appears initially in a simplistic martyr and masochistic form, without connection to the kingly aspect.

Thus one woman who had been rejected in favor of a critically ill brother to whom she was made caretaker at age three and a half, explained that she finally felt she could deserve her depressed mother's love and belong to the family only after suffering a disfiguring accident that gained her a gruesome attention. She said:

> Before that I could never answer my mother's need, so she hated me. But then I became the perfect martyr, the holy one, like Christ, and he even engineered his own end, a deep virtue. The meek will inherit the earth, so I suffer righteously, and that gives me the right to whatever I receive, so I don't have to care; I give up and feel virtuous.

She confused a tyrannical masochism with submission to fate in a magical justification of her own inability to thrive. Her degree of emotional and cognitive incapacity was extreme, but she was still able to hold a job. She entered therapy with the magic belief that anything can be healed. This belief was primarily aimed at the mother she still sought to redeem in order to allow herself "to feel entitled to exist"; it also warded off "terrible grief and horror."

A man who had been abandoned before the age of two by his missionary mother (while she went to further her Christian training) dreamt early in therapy: "I am an infant crucified." He identified with his inner, helpless, mortally wounded child, which had been victimized by a perverted Christianity, and with that child's lonely exaltation as a martyred Christ. He had taken up the burden in his life pattern; he felt himself to be the sick one of the family, responsible for its troubles and therefore severely self-punitive, while also virtuously identifying with the condemning accuser.

Both cases equate the victim, the holocausted aspect of the

scapegoat, with the virtuous martyr. This implies a rejection of all ego assertion, a collusion with the Christianized scapegoater who would make ascetic sheep of the flock to perpetuate a slavish morality. It means an inflation with a distorted image of Christ, one that prevents effective ego development and the individuation potential inherent in the Messiah archetype when it is seen as both scapegoat and king.

The possibility of being inflated with the role of savior, the one who carries away sins as suffering caretaker, is another way in which scapegoat-identified individuals may feel fraudulently Christlike. As one woman explained,

> I did all the suffering in the family. My parents didn't seem to care about the emotional anguish we went through because we moved all the time. I felt it for all of us. Sometimes I wished my sisters could share it so I wouldn't feel so lonely; but I knew I was special.

To this woman, even the feeling of being burdened gave a sense of value and she had many one-sided relationships in which she helped to comfort others. In this way she could care for her own dependency needs in projection, without incurring censure from her negative, condemning animus. "I can split off into caretaking and work so as not to feel pain," she said. "But also in those activities parts of me can at least continue to exist." She had experienced her mother's neglect and had felt responsible for her equally neglected younger sister at a very early age. She had thus developed adult structures precociously over a very unsupported and fragile core. She had not grown into them. She felt she had to "race in and do my job, then race out before anyone finds me out." Since she was deeply identified with the scapegoat as caretaker, she had virtually abandoned her own feeling reactions. She felt omnipotently responsible for all family problems and could not leave the family container to develop her own considerable talents "as long as anyone feels upset; what would they do without me? Especially my mother?"

Initially incapable of acknowledging any personal rage or unfulfilled needs, this woman found defensive meaning and value in playing the savioress. She was unaware that she received some power gratification in infantilizing those she took care of, but she could begin to see that she both wished and feared to be discovered as an infant herself. Working on this, she discovered that she took on others' problems in a magical bargain with God: if she served and held the family problems, then the others, and herself in a primitive symbiosis with them, could live well. "If I sacrifice enough to care for the others, then I'll get care myself." Thus she took on the family pathology in the role of burden-carrying "family therapist"; she felt that worrying a certain amount of time would relieve her mother or a sibling of difficulty.[64] As her mother began finally to take some responsibility for her own life, the young woman was relieved of enough of the suffocating symbiosis to become conscious of her role as scapegoat-redeemer.

A dream then depicted this role as an inflation:

> I am in the kitchen alone. Outside I see a huge balloon over the house. A big clown balloon is attached to it, made to look as if it's supposed to be holding up the round balloon. It's a spoof on God.

In the kitchen she served as family caretaker and servant, the only role she felt she filled competently. To the clown she associated "people with sad lives who make up their faces," and rodeo clowns, who divert the bulls from killing the riders or who "stay at the animal's faces to inflame them because they know the bulls so well." Here the clown balloon serves as "a spoof on God."

Playing with the images of this dream over several months enabled this woman to see that she sought out inflammatory family intensities to provide the excitement of life that she otherwise feared and hid from as the suffering servant. She felt too worthless and rejectable to have a life of her own and too frightened to learn the skills that such a step would require, although she was extraordinarily competent in the service of others. She slowly came to realize that she resented such service, holding up the world like Christ, both God's Fool and *Salvator Mundi*. And she came to see that her sense of the exclusively pained world was itself a balloon to justify her caretaking role. She needed the transpersonal power of her identification to give herself any value at all. While she felt secretly and stubbornly powerful and grand, she did not yet know how to come down to her still very inept finitude.

This woman had not been educated in self-care on earth, and was thus profoundly undeveloped. Identified also with the regressed victim-ego in its overwhelming misery and helplessness, she still sought the all-good savior for herself. She had projected this savior role onto a variety of figures who invariably "betrayed" or "disappointed" her, for part of her secret bargain with God was that if she gave her life for her family, someone would or should appear to serve her equally. This is a common enough distortion of the Messiah archetype, but one that left her in a mix of cruel hope, secret demandingness and abject despair. Until this was confronted in therapy as a coercive system, she could not disengage from her magic caretaking role.

Another young woman had served as family scapegoat and victim of her mother's power complex, feeling blamed for her brother's illnesses and discipline problems among her siblings. As she was beginning to emerge from identification with the scapegoat, she brought a dream that provided a new orientation to her acquired, Sunday-school image of Christ as the passive, righteous martyr:

> I am told about a foreign woman who was given a piece of the left middle square of Jesus to eat after he was crucified. This was usually given to the gravediggers to eat.

To the gravediggers she associated "those who work at night because they do the dirty work no one wants to see; perhaps," she said, "they are also grave robbers." They correspond to her own scapegoat pariah complex that deals with the dirty, shadow stuff unconsciously, and perhaps by stealing what does not belong to it. The part of Jesus to be assimilated in the primitive communion is from the side she said was near his heart and unwounded by the spear. It is the feeling center of Christ, that part which can suffer the opposites and so redeem them.

Through reflecting on these images she was able to distinguish between the abstract, impersonal morality with which she had been brought up, and a still foreign morality to which she might be feelingly and personally related. The issue for her at the time involved a shadow problem with a friend. She could begin to see that its resolution would call forth a new set of nonlegalistic and nonmasochistic values for herself, as well as a new mode of assimilating the opposites and listening to her own conscience.

In this case the appearance of the savior archetype marked the transition toward a capacity for integration of the opposites and transformation. At other times its appearance may be thoroughly regressive. Which way to take the image depends on the person's process, associations and the structure and message of the dream itself.

7

The Feminine and the Year Gods

Individuals caught in the scapegoat complex tend to identify with their weakness and inferiority. They fall victim to the collective shadow, to which they offer themselves with Christ-like atonement. Or they identify with the overburdened Suffering Servant. Thus they play out the role of "man-god slain to take away the sins and misfortunes of the people."[65]

This identification with the dying sacrificial victim and servant leads naturally to a compensatory identification with the reborn Savior King. But in the scapegoat complex, this compensation tends to become split-off, unconscious omnipotence, as discussed above. Together, dying victim and Savior King form the twin motif. That motif is already inherent in the two goats and two gods of the original Hebrew scapegoat ritual.

The archetypal image here is that of the dying and reborn god, originally the consort of the loathesome and beautiful Great Goddess, who grants sovereignty in Vedic, Middle Eastern, African and European mythologies. A human or animal representative of the god was chosen as fertilizing consort of the goddess, then "annually slain for the purpose of maintaining the divine life in perpetual vigor, untainted by the weakness of age."[66] In such rites humans or animals, made sacred and embodying the potency of the god, suffered death and dismemberment in order that the cycle of human and natural life (equated with the Goddess of the Land) be renewed. The Scapegoat, Dying God, Underworld Twin, Old Year or Fool's King are equated with the powers of death, wasteland, drought, darkness, winter and the underworld. The reborn Divine Child, Savior and New King belong with the powers of prosperity, life, health, joy, the fertilizing waters, the renewed sun and renewed rulership.

Such images of the Year God unite the opposites within one containing cycle, and place scapegoat and redeemer in relation to both the process and authority of the Great Goddess of death and rebirth. This wider and older view enables the feminine element, so patently excluded in the Hebrew image (and in the modern scapegoat complex) to be restored. There the feminine occurs only negatively and subordinately, in the mention of the demonic Azazel's teaching women to make cosmetics and in the cultural denigration of qualities considered feminine. But as queen of the land and dispenser of kingship, the Goddess was worshipped in Her own right by pre-Hebraic Semites. Her cults survived in pagan Europe and much of the world. Returning Her to Her primary and life-sustaining place in the original scapegoat pattern provides a context within which the split-off parts of the scapegoat complex can be contained and transformed into aspects of a whole—one containing separateness, even tragic alienation and death, as well as the possibility of community, sovereignty, renewal and life.

For modern women it is crucial that they come to experience the Great Goddess or feminine matrix as a containing wholeness and a support of feminine authority behind the primitive, splitting animus and the life-spoiling effects of the scapegoat complex. Since neither the sky god, Yahweh, nor the demonized Azazel has a positive connection to the feminine, this connection must be discovered in therapy. There the feminine element is basic to the holding environment of the therapeutic vessel in which the healing of the scapegoat complex occurs.

For one woman this discovery came as she worked with a gripping dream:

> An executioner-type bully faces a schoolboy with a little cross on his shirt. It is a stark, and, I fear, doomed encounter for the clean-cut lad. Suddenly I see a very green tree between them, and they both get involved in picking its fruit.

Not satisfied in simply grounding the two animus figures in her personal experience, she drew the image. The tree spread behind the two males as if embracing them. Looking closely at the tree, she saw in it the figure of a woman. She then made a series of drawings of this tree woman, finding that, as the figure emerged more fully, it became large and buxom and full of exuberant life— sometimes dancing, sometimes sitting under a tree or on its branches. She rediscovered the motif of the Goddess in the Tree and the Goddess of the Tree of Life as it appears on ancient cylinder seals. The tree of the original dream and the transpersonal figure derived from it—both symbols of the feminine Self—have enough fruit to sustain both the "good," adaptive and sacrificial sides of life and the brutish power aspects. Work on these images opened a way for this woman to move beyond the imperatives and splits of the complex to a feminine figure with whom she could relate directly. The Goddess in the garden became part of the imaginal life of the dreamer, and through work on other dreams and active imaginations She eventually became a trusted, transpersonal guardian of the lost victim-child in the dreamer's interior world. This eventually enabled the woman to find a sense of personal coherence and empowerment in the outer world.

In scapegoat-identified men the Year God motif may appear in an image of confrontation with a powerful, often threatening and death-like, positive shadow or Self figure. This figure's capacities and libido need to be consciously assimilated. A man must learn to recognize the sadistic accusing animus of the Death Mother, which keeps him identified with rejection, constantly repeating the role of self-sacrificer. The victim-ego sees the "other king" shadow as an awesome and frightening enemy, for its potentially life-enhancing strength and other qualities are initially felt to be alien.

A borderline male patient was caught in "uroboric incest" with a beautiful, destructive mother. In outbursts of animosity she exhorted him to fulfill the expectations of her Azazel animus, and he had internalized these impossible standards. In therapy he came to call them "my accusers." He described his craving for acceptance:

> I want so much to be liked that I adopt others' ways. I'm malleable. I hate and negate myself, whatever that is, and idol-worship anyone who might accept me, but I'm paralyzed around others because they may suddenly turn and reject me.

This man had achieved considerable success in his field but felt he would fail at any moment. He suffered paralyzing anxiety attacks which he imaged as a giant vortex descending to swallow him. Just before starting therapy for the third time he had a dream illustrating the Year King theme in terms of the hostile brothers or golden bough combat motif:

> I am at a public festival. I am led to a cleared area to participate in a dance. A woman in a flowing, beautiful dress stands in the middle of the circle. I am on one side. An iron-muscled man in steel grey with a silver face, like a futuristic warrior, stands on the other side. He is death. The woman dances erotically, beautifully. The dress is the only colored thing in the dream. I get so caught up, I reach to touch the dress or her. Instead, I touch the man. I gasp. People gasp. It happens all over. The third time, I touch the dress and take a piece

of the color in my hand. And then Death is on my back, pressing me down to earth to crush me. I have to start wrestling or die.

On a personal or reductive level this dream is a picture of the man's seductive mother complex which allured and drew him, only to turn its accusing sadistic animus against him. Tantalized, he was held in bondage to the Great Mother as he alternated between clinging victim and rageful omnipotence. In the dream the weak, entranced ego cannot approach the mesmerizing anima. He must first confront the threatening aspect of his masculine shadow. This dark figure will press him to confront the limits of his finite reality. It felt like a death threat to him for he only experienced his potency in outbursts of self-destructive violence, and he feared losing his identity as "hopeless but talented." But in therapy he began to see his connection to a demonic energy that could bless him with masculine strength and discipline as he learned to wrestle with it.

In scapegoat-identified women the Year King motif may occur in the context of searching for and redeeming the positive animus. One dream with such an image was brought by a woman at a significant crisis in her life:

> I am going down a hill, then into a kind of cavern. It's night, very dark. In the cavern I find my brother. I know it's he, although he looks like my son when he was a baby, radiantly beautiful. He lies half under a pile of composting leaves. He had been lost for a while, and I had gone to find him. I pick him up and carry him back up the hill to a huge house where many people with torches await us.

The dream suggests the search of Isis for Osiris, the descent to the underworld made by Damu's mother-sister, and Ishtar's descent to retrieve her dead lover, Tammuz. Here the brother-son had been lost and is found, renewed with infant radiance. He is now the risen Child to be restored to the world of consciousness by the seeking feminine ego. The fertility aspect of death is suggested by the composting leaves, the life that dies to enrich the new field's harvest. Persephone's journey and the torch-lit reception of the new life of Eleusis echo through the dream images.

This woman had been learning to assert herself against the inner Azazel and had also just taken a decisive stand against her scapegoating husband. Her fears of rejection had been re-evoked by her life situation, yet she struggled to find the courage to protect her integrity and creativity, and to free herself from the toils of scapegoat identification. Her brother, she felt, had been the favorite child, a brilliant, creative *puer,* and her inner condemning animus had, until recently, kept a ledger still showing her to be inferior in comparison to him. Now the dream suggests the possibility of the opposites coming together in her psychology, through a descent to the world of the dark feminine where she can find the animus-brother-son, redeemed and reborn. Rather than submitting to the accusing animus, she struggled to claim its strength in order to embrace her own creative potential.

A dream of another woman shows the twin motif in terms of two sisters, both wives of the king. These are seemingly opposed aspects of the feminine which a woman working through the scapegoat complex will inevitably meet and struggle to integrate.

A dark-haired warrior has been fighting to regain his kingship after a long absence. He has two wives, sisters. The first is dark; the second is light and fights alongside the king. He returns finally to the first wife. Their child had left her mother until the father returned. When he returns to the dark wife, the two wives' fortunes together will get the kingship back, and the child can return.

The dreamer identified with the blond, Amazonian wife's appearance and heroic struggling; yet she had always felt herself to be the black sheep of her family, and had adopted a persona of agreeable competence to cover her identification with rejected shadow stuff. The dream occurred as she began to differentiate her personal shadow material from that of the collective and to take responsibility for some aspects of her own, previously repressed, aggression and sexuality.

Here there are two queens, two aspects of the feminine which must cooperate with the warrior attitude to reestablish a long-lost regality. In the dream the heroic animus returns to the dark wife who had waited for him, maintaining his claim at home. She represented for the dreamer the stable order of life and also aspects of the dark feminine. She is to be valued as bearer of a fortune, not neglected as a "discard," identified with values the dreamer had rejected. In the dream the animus's initial connection with the "light" wife is analogous to the dreamer's attempt to evade and repress her chthonic and "conventional" femininity, in order to appear strong, bright, questing and "acceptable." Now the animus, her own potential regality, struggles to return to the neglected, dark queen. For it is with her that the child, the woman's potential for new development, lies. This child can return only when the dark queen is revalued, acknowledged as the carrier of life and the libido necessary to create a new order.

In this woman's case the dark sister was closer to conventionally accepted views of the feminine, for these had been devalued in her identification with the Amazonian fighter. But the "fortunes" of both wives, representing opposite aspects of the feminine, are needed to provide sufficient libido to found the new kingdom.

8

Healing the Scapegoat Complex

Healing the scapegoat complex—disidentifying from it—involves a long process in which each of its parts needs transformation. Some of the specific steps have been suggested above. Ultimately it entails discovery of the transpersonal dimension and validation of an individual wholeness encompassing the oppositions within the complex. Then the relationship to the individual Self provides a secure matrix which relieves one of the need to be bound to the perfectionistic, collective morality that accuses and exiles those who transgress its rules.

This permits moving from a sense of identity split into condemning accuser—alienated, shadow-bearing ego covered by personae—and hidden victim, into a wholeness containing an enduring, asserting, desiring ego sensitive to the unconscious and to the messages of conscience. Knowledge of this new evaluating mode relies on an openness to the Self and its difficult, changing messages—a skill acquired in the process of working through the complex.

Sensitivity and a readiness to take on suffering are already present in the basic character of those individuals who tend to identify with the scapegoat archetype. The capacity to endure and witness, and a willingness to risk change and to play freely with possibilities without shame, are fostered in the healing process through the transference-countertransference, through constant dialogue between conscious and unconscious material, and through encountering the archetypal images and experiencing in life the instinctual dynamisms that coexist with them.

A large part of the initial phase of therapy involves an alliance between analyst and analysand against the accusing scapegoater. When this is strong and the victim-ego feels supported, work can begin toward dismembering and dissolving the defenses of the alienated ego through careful confrontation. This analysis of defenses goes very slowly, for while it often brings relief it is also frightening, since the defenses are experienced as the individual's only conscious identity. When their limits are reached, the emotions walled off within them can flow. Then, as the proud but uneasy strength falls

83

away, the alienated ego finds itself rawly experiencing its exile, feeling again the unhealed wounds and grieving for both the child and the adult burdened with the experience of such pain. Generally this happens through a descent to the wilderness or underworld (perhaps a numbing depression) where the underlying confusion, despair, loneliness, fear and rage are met and suffered, sometimes for months. In this descent there are no available responses from the old levels of effort and will; nor are there easy or collective solutions.[67]

The experience is like that of Inanna on the stake or Christ on the cross. Since it is guided by the Self and companioned by the therapist, the analysand can gradually learn to carry the painful material with feeling and increasing discrimination. Eventually the wounds no longer need to be defended against with automatic guilt, automatic effort and persona omnipotence. As the alienated persona-ego feels defeated, the Self, experienced as guide, support and destiny, can also be met as reality. Then the individual ego, up against the facts of its imperfect life, is permitted to see its true limitations and riches, together with its valid strengths. It is permitted to find and create its personal style, and to discover the voice with which to express its individual experience.

Disidentification from the complex comes about also through parallel but different work with the victim-ego. This part, not yet deintegrated from the archaic Self, begins to experience primal acceptance both through the transference and through the images and affects that come up from the depths of the unconscious. Such acceptance constellates a symbolic or ritualized re-creation of the world of the Mothers, the matrix of life in the maternal, symbiotic Self. This is discovered through the regressive transference. Here the hidden, fixated victim-ego can be found again in its miserable nest of self-hate and related to with caring empathy—an emotion that scapegoat-identified individuals have so rarely experienced toward themselves.

Through the therapist's acceptance and objectivity, and through the inner guidance that informs the psychic process, the negative parental complexes can be transformed. This enables the hidden, true ego to develop. It can discover seeing and being seen objectively. It can learn that action and desire and pain can be held and mirrored, not branded negatively before they are experienced. Such acceptance and objectivity are themselves psychologically nourishing and provide a holding containment in which the pre-ego can learn to endure frustration, to assert, and to accept dependency and independence. Having such a transpersonal and transferential base enables growing beyond the overburdened, initial maternal substitute—the alienated ego, as well as the magic omnipotence of the fixated infant. As one man put it:

> I can feel a home. Rootedness on earth. I get a sense of goodness and strength and passionate intensity as connected to me, so I am not just bad and guilty. I can see myself alive and whole because you see me that way—because you see all of me, not just ugly fragments.

Through this phase of nurturance the victimized one finds experiences and images of inner allies, figures that are objective, protective and respectful. Such figures may be amalgams of dream images, the idealized maternal figure of the symbiotic transference and memories of beloved persons in the past. They supplant the cruel rejectors of the originally constellated scapegoaters.[68]

Because the victim-ego has lived outside of experience, it is unadapted and quite literally uneducated. Often it pushes the therapist to be a model for behaviors and attitudes that need integration. Then the therapist may feel controlled and used, just as the parent of a young child does, in order that the analysand's own process may create what is appropriate for each particular phase of ego development.

> If you can be angry at my parents, I might dare it.

> If you could want me to exist I could use that wanting like a bowl to hold myself in, or an embrace. And I could start to want me too.

Such expressions are calls from the victim-ego to coerce its valid needs from the world of the archetypal parent projected into the therapy.

At other times the therapist is called to withstand the projective identifications of the rejecting scapegoaters. Then the hate, contempt, guilt and other toxins from the complex need to be metabolized and interpreted by the therapist, even while accepting the analysand who is also defending against the therapist as carrier of the projective identification. Only thus can the relative safety of the analytic vessel provide a secure holding environment for the hidden and self-hating child to return to life and grow.

Such experiences permit the individual to pursue assertive energy and desirousness to their life-enhancing and transpersonal origins. Anger can then be recognized as an objective experience of the Self, which stands behind the ego and defends its integrity. Desire can be recognized as based on "the yearning to rest in and be nourished by what is imperishable."[69] The search for a home base, so intense in scapegoat-identified individuals, can be grounded—not in what was behind in early childhood, but in the connection to the transpersonal and a new kin group sharing this experience. Home is created and discovered as a result of one's own work and search. Even pain can be here reevaluated and come to be seen as a part of life, a concomitant of that very vulnerability which allows one to be sensitive. When seen objectively, it is easier not to identify with the pain, but rather to let it come and go as part of the flow of reality.

As the emerging ego begins to disidentify from the scapegoat complex and its old modes of adaptation through the suffering servant role, it can become witness to a reality that is, indeed, part evil. No amount of bearing guilt or atoning can change that fact. Accepting this permits the sacrifice of the innocent, lost child's illusion that "if I'm good enough, then I'll find my corner and Eden will exist for me." It permits sacrifice of the false securities and omnipotence ruled by the accusing Azazel, which were once bought either by identifying with the aggressor or the guilty one or the perfect one, or with the caretaking savior, or by masochistic placation. It permits consciously accepting the sacrifice of an experience of the accepting collective, in order to find one's home in a dynamic and individual relation to a new image of the Self.

This in turn permits sacrificing the habitual self-identifications of the complex and revaluing one's personal history—learning to accept those marks of one's personal style and fate for which one was previously banished by the inner scapegoater. Along the way, there is a series of confrontations with the black and white simplistic values of the old scapegoating demon, together with the struggle to find and embody new conscience-based values—often first represented in dreams by images of criminals and other outcasts. For finally working through the complex means to sacrifice the shallow mode of shadow excision that has been part of the culture, and to accept the task of finding an order based on direct contact with the redeemed images of the transpersonal where Mercy and Justice operate together. This dimension one can serve only in a limited, individual way.

All of these sacrifices permit radical transformation, but they are seldom undertaken out of conscious ego choice. Rather, the scapegoat-identified individual is forced to the depths of the collective unconscious to find there the sources which create and insist on the personal transformation process, and to accept that she or he will always need to be in touch with those sources. For, while healing takes place on different levels and in different degrees, the complex does not disappear. One can only be a "recovered scapegoat." Like a reformed alcoholic, one is forever vulnerable to the building blocks of one's own psychology.

One woman learning to live empathically with the scars and wounding cleavages (that open again under stress severe enough to unsettle the new psychic structures) found she could begin to "mine the black pits." She learned to accept the necessity of each descent to the realms of pain and shadow and to ask its meaning and gift. In a letter two years after leaving analysis she wrote:

> I see I no longer live in the underworld. That's extraordinary itself. But I have to accept that my fate is to fall in occasionally and to grapple with the demons there until I am released. Now I know there's something to get and some real place in life to return to where I can express my experiences and be heard. That's new. And up here I also know that we walk on depths that make each footfall resonate through unseen realms. What a responsibility then to walk and wander, and not to take myself too seriously in the old ways. But what a cursed blessing to have the experiences of that vastness and to know I can survive and share them.

Scapegoat-identified individuals have been devoted to a transpersonal role and carry transpersonal intensities. If they are to serve that role without identifying with its misery and grandiosity, they need other channels into which the released energies can flow. Clinical experience shows that these channels take primarily one of two forms: creative expression into some vessel of art, or initiation into a healing discipline. Both channels permit working at the edge of the collective in order to process the intensities most people cannot bear; and both permit the transpersonal waters to flow in individual patterns.

The artist uses the channels of artistic tradition developed by human cultures over millenia. These can contain and express all manner of intensities. Within the sacred process and with the forms of tradition and personal innovations, the artist can find and create forms which convey individual vision and passion. These expressions serve the collective by mediating what it needs and can bear to see of itself. Even in ways not overtly "artistic," the same energies can be utilized to express the Self's creative intentionality in any and all aspects of life.

Healers are devoted to the wounding and healing energies, helping to channel them toward the release of suffering in others and in themselves. They serve through dealing with the damaged and diseased aspects of individuals and collectives. To the extent that they have found a pattern of wholeness for themselves and are consciously connected to their personal sources of energy, they can facilitate this development in others. The healer can companion the wounded as they, too, learn devotion to the ordering source beyond their painful wounds and fragmentations. Healers can also attend to the recurring open wounds in themselves.

Exiled scapegoats can, thus, return to serve the collective as agents of its deepest and most difficult needs. They serve by mediating the libido necessary to collective and individual life. But they are also a community unto themselves. Like those in the kingdom of the Wayward Princess (see below, page 106), they form a loose society of noncomformists. It is one devoted to the transpersonal processes underlying individuality and the secular collectives. Those in this society listen for the guidance that comes from the intersection of life and death, joy and pain, love and wounding. They are more or less willing to feel its paradoxical and raw nature. Since they struggle continually to accept that intersection in their own hearts, they can work with inevitable shadow projections, not as a prelude to scapegoating and splitting in order to attack, but as a means of lifelong personal growth and ethical actions.

Azazel, The Goat God

Scapegoat-identified individuals can initially see only the unacceptability and darkness of potentially redeeming energies. These are feared and despised, for people identified with the negative shadow see their own identity from the perspective of the accuser.

Not only is their own shadow filled with positive potential, but they overlook much that is life-giving in the negative qualities with which they identify. They feel tabooed, devoted to gods out of favor. But they carry in devalued form a compensation for the collective's one-sidedness. They are "at home with garbage," as one woman put it. She had dreamt that she was searching through an immense garbage dump, picking up many valuable objects. Her finds surprised her, and she remembered Picasso's sculptures created from "bits and pieces he found in the trash." She realized that the garbage she felt herself to be had once been tossed aside carelessly. Now she is asked to sort and humanize it in order for it to become the basis of a new form. The new order does not mean unconscious impulsivity and license. It means both intentionality and improvisation, with personal responsibility to the Self as it guides from within and without, providing the values for each situation and each relationship.

Those identified with the scapegoat cannot initially see the valuable aspects of the rejected stuff because they are enslaved by their exile from and longing to the very collective that banished them. They serve Azazel as he is defined by the Western tradition.

It is important in therapy with such individuals to follow the process of their transformation until it reveals the meaning of Azazel hidden behind the devalued, accusing demon he became in the Judeo-Christian writings. Only then can the fanaticism of the accuser transform into a capacity for passionate service to the transpersonal, while the energies branded evil and carried with shame—and sometimes eruptive ecstasy—become passion for life.

Azazel was originally a divinity symbolized and embodied in the goat, that lively, swift, high-climbing yet earthy, sexually potent animal with a strong odor. It is an animal both combative and nurturant, able to live in inhospitable terrain and willing to be domesticated. As a horned god, the goat is an image of primal creative energy, of generative and destructive force, of desire. As ibex, its form appears on early Sumerian cylinder seals, ritually rampant with the figure of the Great Goddess: the kid with the Mother. There it suggests the instinctive forces of the Great Round, especially those which can be somewhat tamed for human benefit.

The goat was also sacred to a large number of other divinities, from the Sumerian Enki[70] through Pan, Hermes, Aphrodite, Kali, Marduk and Dionysus. All these divinities are associated with the ecstatic depths. They compel, and sometimes mediate, the awesome truth of reality through passionate encounter with affect states that grip the soul and are experienced as transpersonal dismemberments and renewals. They are the states which the laws of Yahweh sought to order and limit. Thus Azazel was posited as the divinity of the place outside Hebrew collective life. He was demoted from his place among the earlier Semites, to whom Azazel was the goat god, a divinity especially honored by herdsmen. He was considered one of the "hairy ones" or Seirim to whom propitiating sacrifices were made.[71] Azazel must also have been similar to his Sumerian counterpart, Ninamaskug,[72] Lord of the Sacred Sheep Stall, shepherd, healer and "psalmist of Enlil." In an ancient Babylonian ritual a man's sickness was poured out at sunset upon the head of a goat dedicated to Ninamaskug, "and the demon parted from the patient."[73]

Azazel then was once a horned and herdsman god of nature,[74] a fertility daimon, a healer, an expression of the creative process in art, and a consort of the Great Goddess, alternating in his office with the farmer god.

All these aspects of the goat god have been lost to Judeo-Christian culture, although they have remained in pagan and folk traditions. Within the dominant stream of culture in the West, the goat is identified with Satan and the demonic energies of the accusing Azazel. This has ensured repression of the qualities the collective rejects. The goat god himself has been made to stand against the very life forces he originally mediated into collective life. As demon and punisher, his image warns away those who would seek him.

In scapegoat-identified individuals' material, the goat often appears after the complex is partially worked through. Awareness of the complex forces a particular set of relations to the horned goat god, as one rediscovers for modern culture the enormous creative energies symbolized in the image. Initially the goat appears as an ambiguous figure. On the one hand it is felt to be excessively wild and untamed impulsivity. It is therefore feared and defended against. On the other hand, it holds creative and erotic potential.

This ambiguity was imaged in the dream of a young woman: "On the main street of town I find a cage. In it a black goat stands with pieces of raw meat around him. My boss keeps the goat there." Her association to raw meat was the frenzy with which the maenads of Dionysus rended live animal flesh. Her association to her boss was rigid, judgmental behaviorism. The dream shows that it is this narrow-minded attitude in her which keeps its opposite—a Dionysian, dismembering impulsivity—penned up. But it is now on "the main street," plainly obvious for her to see. This pair of opposites is analogous to the cultural bifurcation in the figure of Azazel himself. He has been split into demonic, condemning accuser—Yahweh's shadow—and the older, chthonic daimon who instills the passions that sweep through us with godlike autonomy. This division underlies a chronic borderline split in much of Western culture.

In this woman's case, the split Azazel enforced a strong repression, for her consciousness was identified with the judgmental animus against her own needs and assertiveness. At the same time the goat god made her the victim of violent, eruptive rages. The day before the dream she had physically attacked her husband, displacing fury at her boss and father onto him. Reflecting on the images of the dream, she began to heal the split. She saw that the repressor she served and hated was the source of the very ecstatic fury she loved and feared—and felt toward that bullying, repressive animus and the men in her life on whom she projected it. Her emotions toward repressor and impulsivity were at the same pitch, just as repressor and passion were both Azazel.

Exploring her eruptive anger, she found it was often rationalized by identification with the accuser's ideals. She explained:

> I get gratified by my rage at subverted ideals. I even hang onto what disappoints me to feed off the anger. The power of the rage is gripping. It may be fairly impotent outside, but it fills me up, so I don't even notice that I don't really care about all those perfect standards and certainties. And I don't even notice that I'm being deflected from claiming my own life.

While she served both sides of the split Azazel, she could begin to see that she maintained high standards (specifically for her husband) in order to fuel her ecstatic rage. The ideals of the accuser began to be less significant than the sense of her own inner space filling up from the emotion. As in many such instances, this form of self-feeding off intense affect was established as an addictive habit in her severely neglected infancy.

About two years later, after a dramatic confrontation with her employer in which she stood up to his fanatic righteousness but felt uncertain of herself afterward, she dreamt again of a goat: "I am in a woods. A man with a face like a goat approaches me across a stream and hands me an old brass lamp. I know it is valuable."

Here the goat image is not raw, caged impulsivity. The assertive instinct has been humanized. It is the bringer of a lamp, consciousness that is ancient but new to her and "from the other side of the stream"—from the unconscious. The goat-faced man approaches her with deliberation and respect, and he offers a gift. In active imagination with this figure she learned that he brought her a new way of evaluating experience, a new wisdom, one in touch with the moment and affirming her own feminine, instinctual reactions. He became an important guide for her through the next phase of her analytic process, as she learned to trust her own instincts.

Partly because of the innate sensitivity of scapegoat-identified individuals, and partly because the ego has remained so long in hiding—close to the archaic Self and not yet deintegrated—these persons have a capacity for emotional intensity that initially seems frightening. As one woman said, "Both joy and sorrow frighten me, as if I still have the raw intensity of a child. I feel everything almost too hard. It's almost a curse."

The intensity is partly the result of the pressure of unconscious, hence compulsive, energies clamoring for release. But ultimately the rush of instinctive energy symbolized by the goat has a transpersonal basis, and the scapegoat-identified individual does not easily or ever fully give it up. For the impulsivity maintains the instinct as a pure visitation of godlike energy which has a power commensurate to the power of the repressive Azazel. While the pre-ego is fearful before unleashed greed and rage, there is paradoxically an aversion to taming such force. There is a clear sense that the exciting rush of spontaneous energy is numinous and to be safeguarded. It compensates the meaninglessness of the wilderness. The same woman who expressed her fear of joy and sorrow said:

> When my greed or rage come out, it's unplanned, wonderful. I don't know what to do with it, but it's present and I trust it, it can't be put down. I refuse to hold back, though I know it's stupid and "infantile instant gratification." I always like the movies where the horse breaks free and goes back to being a wild stallion, refuses to be broken. It keeps its integrity. That's the only level I believe in.

This woman sensed the drama of the confrontation between the forces of repressive, collective controls and the untamed life force which alone could burst what she called "the cage of false definitions and rules." The possibility of taming such energy, finding appropriate measures and strategies to release the passion, seemed only like acquiescing in its destruction, being "broken." Her accusing animus strove to repress all relation to her affects, but she felt their numinous power and was herself split in her allegiance. She served both the Yahwistic Azazel and the pre-Hebraic goat god, identifying with one or the other, but unconsciously.

Later she found that the chthonic Azazel has its own instinctive self-controls. As she learned that she did not have to panic at every discomfort, she could to some extent contain and mediate her own reactions. At the same time she began to ask for what she needed and to trust that she might receive gratification. This strengthening of her ego both freed her desirousness and was accompanied by a confidence in its discipline. After a session in which she verbally expressed erotic feelings for the therapist and wondered at the absence of shame in herself, she dreamt:

> I am in a shower stall. A very hairy man watches me pull on my clothes. He runs toward me aroused, his penis erect. I fear he will rape me and tell him, No. He stops running, and we confront each other.

The hairy, ithyphallic figure reminded the dreamer of Pan. Here the concrete, physical, erotic, spontaneous, creative—all that the goat-god heralds—is still feared, but it approaches the dreamer and does not overwhelm her. The shower represents a freeing baptism into new understanding, a new relation to her own instinctual compulsivity. She finds that it is a strong and aroused passion but one that respects discipline and inhibition. Hence it has a creative potential. The dream initiated a sexual responsiveness in her marriage that the dreamer had not known before, and also her return to a long dormant artistic talent.

After several years of therapy, a man who had imagined his split between a dour minister and a passionate berserker, and could give up neither of them, brought a dream:

> I am in a cave where a woman sits over a crack in the earth. Fumes come out of it and she rants, beautiful, but I can't understand her. A priest turns to tell me what she is saying.

He remembered Lagerqvist's novel, *Sibyl,* but he was struck in the dream by the potency of the image of the priest, who can interpret the sibyl's ravings as she is possessed by the goat god. The sibyl is overcome ecstatically by fumes from the earth, as the patient felt overcome by his bursts of impulsivity. But her messages are needed by the human supplicants, and there is the possibility of a new reverential, priestly attitude that can serve the life-giving incoherent force and try to mediate it into humanly related modalities, into effectively expressed feeling reactions.

A woman once deeply caught in the scapegoat complex also

encountered the goat god at a transition point where the image appeared as a guide to a new relation to her Self's feminine authority. After an initiatory ordeal which she felt she had barely survived, she made an "automatic drawing"—an active imagination—to try to express the intensity of her experience. Looking at the paper afterward, she saw that it depicted a goat head that also looked like a Menorah, the Jewish tree of life and lights. In the branches of the tree were three suns or eyes. In the roots was a fourth dark sun which served as mouth. She imagined it talking and heard deep tones that filled her with awe. That night she dreamt of a headless man in green who approached across a bridge carrying this same "goat-tree-head" under his arm. To this figure she associated the Green Knight of Celtic myth, the god symbolizing transformation and the enduring potency of nature, who initiated the hero with the greatest courage and integrity according to the plans of the Goddess he served. In this woman's psychology, the figure imaged a radical transformation in her animus—one implying the relativization of heroic, intellectual and obsessive controls, together with a new spontaneity and trust of the Self's depths. In a series of meditations and active imagination with the mysterious figure, she found that he could serve her as a psychopomp, initiating her into a new mode of creative self-expression and a new career, one in which service to the Self was respected.

In the creation of this new order lies the meaning of the dying and reborn fertility spirit as it is encountered in individuals caught in the scapegoat complex. Such persons suffer exile and holocaust, caught in the split-off one-sidedness and black and white moralisms of the demonic condemning Azazel.

As the victim-ego is discovered behind the defenses of the alienated persona and allied with, held in the analytic vessel and mirrored with a new kind of attention from both the analyst and the dream images, it can learn a new mode of witnessing as consciousness. It can begin to look at the demonic accusations and weigh them from a new center of assessment. The contemptuous, accusatory perfectionism of the demonic Azazel can, thus, transform into an ego capacity for critical differentiation of carefully witnessed events. As the ego relates from its new center of authority and feels itself capable of discriminating objectively, the crust of righteous accusatoriness that had frozen negatively judged emotionality can then also change—often indicated by dream images of melting ice.

The ecstatic potential symbolized by the goat god can then find release in newly discovered forms.

A dream presaging this shift came from a woman whose fundamentalist background had made all passion sinful, except that righteous indignation in which her parents indulged. She dreamt that she was in her therapy group, noticing the subtle shifts of tones as people spoke. Then the door opened and some mummers entered. Her first reaction was fear, but she noticed that they brought bagpipes and were dancing. Two of them grabbed her up and she started tentatively to dance with them, trying to discover steps that would fit the new music. She felt self-conscious as the rest of the group watched, but she soon got caught up in the dancing and found she could enjoy herself.

The mummers suggest the ancient solstice dramas in which the powers of light battle those of darkness, with a priest or druid assisting to restore the world to light and warmth.[75] It was by attending to a level of sound different from verbal communication that the dreamer opened her inner door to the influx of this new element. By going beyond the judgmentalism, which initially made her self-conscious, she was able to experience her spontaneity and truly join the dance.

From the perspective of the scapegoat complex, Azazel is the divinity representing both the disorder of impulsivity and the severe condemnations of impulse. Thus he provides an archetypal image for the carrier of these opposites. As he is redeemed through therapeutic work on the splits engendered in the complex, these opposites can be carried as ambivalence. The goat god can then symbolize the capacity to mediate ecstasy and discipline, playful improvisation and serious work—providing the basis for creativity. When the instinctual energy can be endured and balanced with its own inhibition, it is seen to be the previously unlived wisdom and creativity of the horned divinity, the chthonic shadow or animus redeemed. Working through the scapegoat complex thus inevitably brings the individual to the horned god at its archetypal core, even as it redeems that god. From a devalued nature spirit onto which Jehovah's shadow was projected, perverting it to a carrier of abstract, impersonal legalism, the goat god becomes instead the symbol of a source of new, spontaneous life that can relate to pleasure and play, the sensuousness of the body and earthy experiences. Azazel becomes the spirit guide that can relate the ego to the depths and heights. The passionate intensity that had been perverted in the accuser can then become the capacity to focus objectively and a passionate intensity for life and spirit—an objective passion that is like "an Eros for Logos."[76]

The libido symbolized by the goat dedicated to Azazel becomes energy that can be devoted to creativity and exploration outside collective constraints, yet sensitive to them and willing to bear the consequences of going its own way. Such originality will earn gratitude from the collective as well as envious hostility. Both need to be borne as this energy impels the individual to seek the spirit in genuine nonconformity to the collective.

As the Strong One of God, then, Azazel presents an image for carrying the ordeals of life, its confusions, its inevitable oppositions. Rather than evading the shadow and excising it with scapegoating and persona goodness, or accepting a collective identity by merging with the scapegoat role, we can learn to see the darkness as part of the *tragoedia,* the goat song, a hymn to the gods. From that perspective the engagement with evil, the suffering and shame of the ego's passion and defeat, and the rebirth on another level—where the Self is manifest as individual wholeness encompassing the opposites—all these are stages in the process of individuation.[77]

The Priest of Yahweh

In the scapegoat complex Yahweh is split from his own chthonic energy and the coherent and differentiated, cyclic forms of instinctual life symbolized by the goat god. In astrological tradition Yahweh is connected with the planet Saturn, ruler of the energies that bind, limit, crystalize, order, discipline and form life structures. In the complex these Saturnian qualities of limitation are negativized to galling inhibition, petrification and sterility. They create the rigidified and abstract, perfectionistic forms that nature cannot bear, and which are projected onto the demonic Azazel.

As the complex is healed, the Saturnian qualities can be felt also as positive limitations and ego ideals, not divorced from nature and the instinctive levels of human existence. Not only does this relieve Azazel of the negative Saturnian shadow, but it also transforms the image of Yahweh. He then becomes the god of individual calling, of individual intention and constructive limitation—the god of "I am that I am." He represents differentiated consciousness within the world of nature and human nature.

As Saturn, Yahweh is ruler of the astrological sign Capricorn, the goat-fish. Azazel as goat god is also Capricorn. On this deeper esoteric matrix, the split of the complex is healed. Yahweh and Azazel become aspects of the One—sky god and horned god, both necessary and in balance if differentiated, abstract order and instinctuality are to thrive in men and women.

The repressive superego also transforms, becoming a capacity for self-discipline and both the binding focus and the ego goals which permit intentionality. The priest of Yahweh, a voice speaking for multitudinous collective imperatives in the complex, is restored to his sacred duty. The priest—or priestess—instead interprets and mediates in service to the Self. It becomes a psychic function enabling one to find and follow the voice of genuine conscience, the autonomous psychic factor which often runs counter to the collective moral code.

Thus the priestly function aids us in making atonement with our own ordering center. As individuals we may then find our way between conflicting imperatives—by sacrificing our ego's stake in serving any of them, by enduring the experience of the painful limits of ego capacity and the frustrations of reality, and by suffering a kind of psychic relativization as we recognize the paradoxes of the whole situation, both inwardly and outwardly. We can be restored to a sense of harmony, find our atonement with our individual Self through the transpersonal nature of conscience itself. As Jung writes:

A creative solution emerges which is produced by the constellated archetype and possesses that compelling authority not unjustly characterized as the voice of God. The nature of the solution is in accord with the deepest foundations of the personality as well as with its wholeness; it embraces conscious and unconscious and therefore transcends the ego.[78]

9

The Meaning of the Scapegoat Archetype

The scapegoat phenomenon is a particular expression, along with Cain, Ishmael, Satan, witch-hunting, minority persecution and war, of the general problem of shadow projection. It is, as we know from anthropological data, an almost universal phenomenon. In cultures where conscious connection to the transpersonal source has not been lost, the one identified with the scapegoat serves the community by returning evil to its archetypal source through sacrifice, carrying back to the gods a burden too great for the human collective to bear. In Western culture, those who suffer identification with the archetype share the burden of the central divinity of our eon, for the archetype of the Messiah as Suffering Servant is at the core of the Western psyche. We all feel its power and share its effects to some extent.

When in the modern age individuals are deeply identified with the role of the scapegoat, they suffer the symptoms discussed above—they endure negative inflation, exile and splitting. They are cut off from an adequate relation to the outer world and to their own inner depths. But even after they are able to disidentify from the burden of the complex, they have a special relation to the archetype. "The complex becomes a focus of life,"[79] for their personalities have been built within its pattern. Thus they are "called" to carry the complex consciously. These individuals are left with a need to discover and relate consciously to its specific meaning in their lives. In this search and service is their healing.

Such service implies a conscious relation to one's own wounds, those places of shame wherein the scapegoat-identified individual felt the pain of being a pariah, cut off from the Self still projected onto the parental container. These wounds turned initially into the scar tissue that perpetuated unconscious splitting and the further loss of relations to the external collective and the transpersonal. Through conscious sacrifice of the inflated, collective identity as scapegoat and savior, these wounds can better be borne openly—suffered as open conflicts between the voice of the collective and the messages of the individual Self. Just as the spear wound in Christ's side was seen to be the womb of the Church, so these wounds can be seen as the vessel of one's own individual soul, bringing forth the individual as one is destined to be. One's vulnerability is seen then as a service to life.

This restored sense of wholeness permits leaving the collective to go forth consciously and with conscience, bearing some measure of one's own shadow. Jung has stressed that struggling with one's own shadow permits a degree of self-reliance and psychological autonomy, an enlargement of consciousness, the sacrifice of the ideal of perfection for one of wholeness, and some relativization of good and evil—clearly necessary if we are all to live on one planet. Erich Neumann further suggests that bearing one's own shadow liberates the collective:

> In contrast to scapegoat psychology, in which the individual eliminates his own evil by projecting it onto the weaker brethren, we now find that the exact opposite is happening: we encounter the phenomenon of "vicarious suffering." The individual assumes personal responsibility for part of the burden of the collective, and he decontaminates this evil by integrating it into his own inner process of transformation. If the operation is successful, it leads to an inner liberation of the collective, which in part at least is redeemed from this evil.[80]

One young woman brought a dream which imaged her as one who relieved the collective of its shadow material. She had been in therapy for five years and had just returned from a visit to her sanctimonious parental home, depressed and regressively identified with her victimized ego. She dreamt:

> I am walking through my parents' house. It's also like my grandparents' house. It's a mess. I seem to have a pile of their old garbage that I have to carry out. I find a pit outside the back door. It's a large, lead-lined hole in the ground.

She associated the garbage to the anger she had felt when her minister father had humiliated her children and dominated their activities in order to enhance his persona before his parishioners. She had expressed her feelings, but she had not felt them understood. She knew consciously that she felt her children's treatment so poignantly because it reminded her of countless experiences of her own with her father. She was aware of his human limitations and even of what she called his "pious-preacher's dissociation." She knew she had been the family scapegoat and had felt the family power-shadow keenly. Now this dream brought the new realization that her rage was not hers alone, but part of the ancestral shadow that she had been handed to deal with.

Because the garbage pit had a lead lining, she thought the waste materials must be radioactive. She mused:

> It can't be put safely into the air, the water, or the earth. All that ministerial power stuff, that rage. It's too potent. What is that lead-lined container for me?

We had talked about her own old schizoid defenses as an inert, unfeeling containment. She had originally imaged them as a "leaden façade." The garbage pit was a variation on the theme, but it was open and already grounded. She decided it referred to the psycho-dramatic and ritualized enactments of her rage that she had performed earlier in her analysis. Spontaneously she picked up a piece of driftwood in the office and, using it like a dagger, she began to move. With increasing fury she danced. When she was done, she glowed—her own life energy had returned. She explained that she had done the dance of Jael, the Kenite heroine in the Old Testament. By connecting to an archetypal image of murderousness and express-ing its dark affect, she was able to carry forward the dream and contain the collective shadow impulse within a ritual and aesthetic form.

Further reflection on the image of Jael showed us that it was a particularly apt one. It mirrored precisely the woman's experience of the ancestral dissociation, but in a redeemed and conscious form. Jael lured the enemy general, Sisera, with milk and offers of protec-tion in order to murder him. Yet she is honored. In the Song of Deborah she is called "blessed . . . among women . . . among all women that dwell in tents may she be blessed."[81] The patient's parents covered their psychologically murderous power urge with a veneer of pious goodness and hospitality. The woman herself had identified with the innocent persona; and, split off from her aggres-sive libido, she had also identified with her victim-ego. The active imagination in ritual dance made conscious and reintegrated the shadow energies, relativizing both persona and shadow within a strong, feminine Self image, one which could carry the ancestral garbage.

Such a conscious suffering of the collective power shadow not only somewhat liberated those in her immediate environment, but also gradually made this woman "psychologically noninfectious."[82] She became increasingly able to confront her parents and others without becoming infected by their anger. She also became able to deal in her relationships with conscious, adaptive assertiveness instead of poisoning contagious resentment.

Just as the priest of the Yoruba smallpox cult, who alone treats patients of the disease, is himself recovered from the disease and therefore immune, so the individual disidentified from the scapegoat complex can confront similar wounds and guilt in others and become an agent of consciousness and healing. The dream of one man who went on to become an analyst illustrates how the process of disidentification served to permit his becoming a healer. He dreamt:

> I am in France where I find a medieval city that is now modernized, the old churches surrounded by modern houses. There are many individual styles among the architecture. There is also a display of the only type of architecture not permitted—a windowless arched cave, which has a bloated, big-headed dummy male figure in it, like a diver who lives off piped supplies. I show the friends I am with, and we agree that is a horrible way to live. I meet my woman friend. She has finished medical school. We decide to leave the town to go into the desert. She doesn't want to come until I persuade her that we can write a new *materia medica* for desert life. She accepts because that is a sufficient life challenge.

To France, this man associated a beloved aunt and his conversations with her, one of the few early places his feelings ever flowed. The medieval walled city (the complex—a defended place of clear-cut collective virtue and vice) has been modernized: each individual is given the possibility of a uniquely designed psychic space within the whole. The diverse aspects of the dreamer have space and are accepted. Only the old encapsulating schizoid defensiveness is forbidden. The dreamer felt the cave to be an image of his old fear of loneliness. It was the primary symptom of his scapegoat complex. To the dummy he associated his mindless accommodating posture that needed "piped supplies" because he couldn't relate humanly and directly. But more positively, the dummy also suggested the idea of being a "psychological diver," an explorer of the unconscious.

In the lysis of the dream, accepting the loneliness consciously becomes the cure: the dreamer and his healer-anima sacrifice the collective life and willingly go into the wilderness to discover a new healing repertoire. Consciously consenting to the individuation potential within the archetype becomes a life's work; the pathology suffered through and borne consciously becomes a calling to serve—

not in the old collectively appeasing ways, but as a wounded-healer who dares to venture beyond the collective walls to where the Self calls. As this man finally reconciled to his fate put it:

> My parents sent me away so I could learn the feeling way that they could never teach me. But now in their old age they need it and so do many others. They seek me out. I feel like the Prodigal Son. It almost makes the exile years seem a destined misery that I could grow from.

The wilderness, here entered consciously, expresses the scapegoat's true relation to the gods. Through alienation from the collective, the scapegoat serves in a medial capacity, helping to connect the world of consciousness to that of the objective psyche. Such service to the transpersonal requires an heroic and conscious venturing into the otherworld, places considered evil, archaic, terrible—those very wilderness regions that were originally the scapegoat-identified individual's personal hell, but where now the numinous energies can be met with the new attitudes born through the transformation process.

The scapegoat is one of many images that suggest the interface between consciousness and unconsciousness. Along with artists, priests, shamans, clowns and witches, the scapegoat crosses the boundary of the collective and deals with material too fraught with danger and chaos for ordinary secular hands. Along with these others the scapegoat serves to redeem the old modalities, specifically by having to confront and struggle with the material repressed by the culture.

The "be ye perfect" enjoinder of the demonic accuser loses its distorted and exoteric meaning as an imperative to live up to collective behavioral standards. It becomes instead an invitation to the service of the spirit as it manifests individually to a deeply attuned consciousness. It becomes a call to discover this inherent mode of knowledge—initially by the very task of "working through" the scapegoat complex itself. It becomes a call to discover the destiny which granted this painful role as an awakener of the redeeming spirit within.

Here psychotherapy takes its rightful place as a steppingstone toward the knowledge of the individual's true essence—the Self—and the meaning of one's current fate on earth.

A remarkable dream of another woman, who was working her way out of the complex, presents an image of the profound process by which she was taught about the transpersonal source of good and evil:

> My father is drunk. I am running young slaves across the border, hiding them on the deck of slow boats that are moving north. I take them to homes where they will be safe, like Harriet Tubman did. I find a pit near the river to shit and fill it with my usual mega-colon bowel movement. . . . Then I am in a pool where there is a man like Einstein who has been sent to tell me about cosmology and the mysteries of the world. I listen and swim. He speaks of training people to go to the heavenly bodies where disease starts, to see about what causes it, how it is kept there. There is something to learn about transport. There is a paradox: space is nothingness, empty, yet it has these bodies/planets where disease originates. A woman there says the theory will not come for a couple of years. The man was sent to talk just to me but now there are a lot of officials around. Someone says that what I missed will be explained in a journal of our new society.

Here the father principle is depotentiated and unconscious. The patriarchal animus is no longer condemning. Thus the repressed emotionality, passion and relation to nature, which the dreamer associated to the slaves, can start to move toward freedom. The dream ego acts with the psychopomp Self figure in the underground railroad to free the oppressed shadow. In the process the dreamer can relieve herself of the massive accumulation of impacted aggression—the resentment she had built up as dutiful family scapegoat.

Then, like a baptism, a new archetypal perspective is opened to her. The extraordinary messenger reveals that disease and evil have a transpersonal source. They belong to the universe, not to her personally. But she is to be involved in the process of comprehending this dark side of cosmic life as part of a developing new dimension of consciousness, a new society. In the dream there are mysteries of "transport," which she explained were "due to centrifugal force, so a special essence carrying people can flow from one cosmic body to another." This image suggested to her that the energy generated by recircling the life problem, through her analysis and her introversion, could permit human consciousness to make the intuitive leap necessary to explore the divine paradox: that out of Nothingness come spheres of matter-energy-awareness that create pain. This suggests a modern equivalent of Buddha's vision. Just as *avidja* (self-delusion) is the cause of suffering, so it is that the partial and distorted consciousness inherent in the complexes we are destined to bear causes dis-ease. Only through the "transport" between these complexes, accomplished by circumambulating the Self's wholeness pattern, can we find the meaning to relativize inevitable human suffering. Evil can thus be seen as related to its transpersonal source.

Service to the scapegoat archetype also serves to differentiate evil, to discriminate between levels of the shadow. Here is a woman's dream that illustrates the need to be aware of the difference between personal, collective and archetypal shadow contents:

> I have cleaned out my drainpipe and then follow it outside. It leads me to a fertilizer factory. There are pipes from each house in town. All the drainage and shit goes into three large drums and is heated up. Then it gets shoveled out as manure to make the farms fertile. There is some left over in the drums—a dark residue. That gets piped through a special direct tube into a hole in the sea.

This woman had discovered that she could not get a revered mentor to accept her when she felt hatred. The hot rage had freed her ego from the idealizing transference and permitted her a view of an alternative mode of handling the unacceptable emotion. She could relate to it consciously and sort out her feelings, even accept some of the shadow from which her mentor turned away. The strong affects could be used as fertilizer for her environment, to make things grow, when she expressed them in dehydrated, conscious form. Some of her resentment was a valid and collective stand against a shallow, sentimental whitewashing of reality. But the deepest residue of the collective shit must go back, as the dream indicates, into the unconscious. Like the ring in Germanic legend and Tolkein's trilogy, such libido is too much to bear and needs to be returned to the unconscious, to the gods. It will return in some new form, for libido does not vanish. But it cannot be borne by the individual or by the collective. It cannot be redeemed or changed to detoxify it by any merely human control.

This distinction in levels of the collective shadow is analogous to that made in the occult tradition between relative and absolute evil. There is a part of the shadow that is culturally relative, which when made conscious can be revalued and returned to enrich the collective. There is also an abysmal, even willful destructiveness which would turn against cultural evolution and the gods themselves. This is absolute evil, part of some incomprehensible malevolence and power before which, like Job, we can only cover our mouths when we see it in nature and glimmering darkly in ourselves.

The woman mentioned above saw her hatred of life and destructiveness as related to the energies which produced the concentration camps, as well as to the energies that erupt from the depths of psychosis. Like all scapegoat-identified individuals, she too readily took excessive personal responsibility for these aspects of the collective shadow. She had in fact spent her earlier life in service to causes and in helping others. For her the black hole in the sea seemed connected to the depths of terrible powers—the cleft of Mordor, the archaic, primeval tomb—a black hole which focuses the ineluctable destructiveness of unrelated Being, that darkest coldness. In the dream she could see it was transpersonal.

Looking into the maw of this fierce, fearsome place of power has a dual effect. It is not only tomb, it is also womb. It releases the individual to a new birth. One's own hatred and destructiveness can be seen as a reflection of the dark side of the transpersonal, which for individuals identified with the scapegoat is a necessary affirmation. The shadow energies with which they have been identified, ultimately even the hate and destructiveness they feel, are reflections of the dark side of existence. They can be claimed consciously as affirmations of wholeness and of the Self's capacity to bring forth in each of us our own monstrous individuality. But, besides this, recognition of the awesome places of power forces us to take a personal stand. We come into ourselves as we wrestle with the dark energies surging through us and through others, as we learn to stand consciously against the mere acting out of the powers in which we, each of us, partake.

The ancient scapegoat rite stands at the periodic transitions which usher in the New Year. It is a foundation sacrifice to propitiate the divinity and ensure divine protection of the new phase or form of cultural life. The widespread evidence in our time of injury to the deepest and earliest layers of the psyche, and of alienation and rejection-inferiority complexes, suggests that a new age is in preparation, and that we as individuals suffer its formation. Exile from the original nurturing container, concretized in the family collective, is a commonplace in our age.

Such consciousness can only be served individually. Each person destined to become a conscious individual by virtue of exile from the collective comes to a particular view and relation to this consciousness—one fostered in part through one's own life wounds and particular kind of exile. Those who come to this awareness are the builders of a new temple and a new kingdom.[83]

There is a Sufi story that was brought to my attention independently by three analysands identified with the scapegoat archetype. It expresses the positive meaning of the scapegoat as the carrier of a new order.

The Wayward Princess

A certain king believed that what he had been taught, and what he believed, was right. In many ways he was a just man, but he was one whose ideas were limited.

One day he said to his three daughters:

"All that I have is yours or will be yours. Through me you obtained your life. It is my will which determines your future, and hence determines your fate."

Dutifully, and quite persuaded of the truth of this, two of the girls agreed.

The third daughter, however, said:

"Although my position demands that I be obedient to the laws, I cannot believe that my fate must always be determined by your opinions."

"We shall see about that," said the king.

He ordered her to be imprisoned in a small cell, where she languished for years. Meanwhile the king and his obedient daughters spent freely of the wealth which would otherwise have been expended upon her.

The king said to himself:

"This girl lies in prison not by her own will, but by mine. This proves, sufficiently for any logical mind, that it is *my* will, not hers which is determining her fate."

The people of the country, hearing of their princess's situation, said to one another:

"She must have done or said something very wrong for a monarch, with whom we find no fault, to treat his own flesh and blood so." For they had not arrived at the point where they felt the need to dispute the king's assumption of rightness in everything.

From time to time the king visited the girl. Although she was pale and weakened from her imprisonment, she refused to change her attitude.

Finally the king's patience came to an end.

"Your continued defiance," he said to her, "will only annoy me further, and seem to weaken my rights, if you stay within my realms. I could kill you; but I am merciful. I therefore banish you into the wilderness adjoining my territory. This is a wilderness, inhabited only by wild beasts and such eccentric outcasts who cannot survive in our rational society. There you will soon discover whether you can have an existence apart from that of your family; and, if you can, whether you prefer it to ours."

His decree was at once obeyed, and she was conveyed to the borders of the kingdom. The princess found herself set loose in a wild land which bore little resemblance to the sheltered surroundings of her upbringing. But she soon learned that a cave would serve for a house, that nuts and fruit came from trees as well as from golden plates, that warmth came from the Sun. This wilderness had a climate and a way of existing of its own.

After some time she had so ordered her life that she had water from springs, vegetables from the earth, fire from a smouldering tree.

"Here," she said to herself, "is a life whose elements belong together, form a completeness, yet neither individually nor collectively do they obey the commands of my father the king."

One day a lost traveller—as it happened a man of great riches and ingenuity—came upon the exiled princess, fell in love with her, and took her back to his own country, where they were married.

After a space of time, the two decided to return to the wilderness where they built a huge and prosperous city where their wisdom, resources and faith were expressed to their fullest possible extent. The "eccentrics" and other outcasts, many of them thought to be madmen, harmonized completely and usefully with this many-sided life.

The city and its surrounding countryside became renowned throughout the entire world. It was not long before its power and beauty far outshone that of the realm of the princess's father.

By the unanimous choice of the inhabitants, the princess and her husband were elected to the joint monarchy of this new and ideal kingdom.

At length the king decided to visit the strange and mysterious place which had sprung up in a wilderness, and which was, he heard, peopled at least in part by those whom he and his like despised.

As, with bowed head, he slowly approached the foot of the throne upon which the young couple sat and raised his eyes to meet those whose repute of justice, prosperity and understanding far exceeded his own, he was able to catch the murmured words of his daughter:

"You see, Father, every man and woman has his own fate and his own choice."[84]

In the tale exile provides an impetus to re-sort, reconcile and redeem the old value system, and permits the establishment of a new kingdom. In this new kingdom the old collective values are left behind—not killed or rebelled against, but simply abandoned, outgrown. And the new kingdom is set up in the wilderness—the in-between place where wanderers and "eccentrics" dwell. The wilderness, an image so frequent in scapegoat-identified individuals' dreams, becomes finally an image of the interface, a ground from which the stable ego can actively seek out a creative relation to the ever-present breadths and depths of the objective psyche.

Radically new in this vision is the respect of each individual for the particularity of another's views and contribution. As one woman put it:

> Because I can love my own scars and my strengths now—care about them and parent them—I can even love my own fate. Also I can accept the wounds and strengths in others and forgo needing to be the one who is right and powerful or the one who is wrong and disgustingly weak. We are each right, and each wrong, like the blind men with the elephant. Because we each have a piece of the truth. The truth is there but we are each limited to our own limited view. So we need each other and complement each other.

The scapegoat problem admits of no easy resolution in collective culture. The spirit of all groups is prone to magic-level consciousness, with its propensity for splitting and shadow projection. Most groups retain their shared sense of positive identity by coalescing against an adversary—thrusting out what is felt to be negative—just as most individuals do.[85] But the type of consciousness that permits witnessing this fact is not a characteristic of the primitive group spirit. It must be deliberately fostered. It can only be carried by individuals, and unless there is respect for individual perspectives within the group, the gadfly voices crying in the collective wilderness may go undifferentiated.[86] Objective witnesses cannot then be discriminated from unadapted cranks, self-seekers and unconscious borderline characters who thrive off the oppositionalism that fills their own power needs. Too often the authoritarian hierarchy of the group exacerbates the inherent difficulty of differentiation and quells potentially creative dissent.

The archetype of the scapegoat itself can mediate between a coherent, positively-identified group and outsiders, just as it mediates between individual ego ideals and shadow—by making conscious the meaning and dynamics of shadow projection. However, unless the archetype is carried with the consciousness that permits disidentification, it will mire group members and the group spirit in splits similar to those sufffered by individuals. In order for the archetype to be carried with consciousness, it needs a meaningful image that can contain its splits and hold a mirror up to its own nature.

While Christ is for many Christians merely another scapegoat who will bear all of the believer's sins, from an introverted, spiritual perspective he may be seen as the symbol of one who bears the suffering of the inner opposites consciously, as his personal crucifixion. In this sense he is a model for the individuating ego, which bears its wholeness as undefensively—and hence consciously—as possible.[87] This implies accepting qualities that match the ego ideal as well as those that fall short of it, holding the opposites together simultaneously, with thought and intuition, in order to perceive one's self-image. This permits a disconcerting and sobering view of the paradoxes, sonorities and dissonances of one's own nature.

An equally meaningful symbol enabling consciousness of these oppositions from a feminine, feeling and rhythmically alternating perspective may be found in images of the Great Goddess (e.g., Inanna, Persephone, Kali, Isis, etc.). These express ideal and shadow aspects of the whole, balancing through time. Thus Inanna is sometimes life-promoting, sometimes ruthlessly destructive; Kali is sometimes maternal and sometimes savagely devouring. They symbolize a model that permits the individuating ego to experience both sides, or many sides, of its nature with emotional intensity, and to remember them all as they manifest on the paradox-containing ground of time behind the divergences. This model, because it depends on the integrity of embodied and affectual perception, is time-bound.

Both of these symbolic patterns imply the necessity to come to an awareness of the ground of reality behind the opposites. They suggest the spiritual awareness of the tree of life and death, which in legend lies hidden from all but the initiates, encircled behind the tree of the knowledge of good and evil. To arrive at such awareness involves a transformation in one's perception of the godhead itself. This transformation is implicit in the healing of the scapegoat complex, for the function of the two goats, sacrificed to atone with the divinity, is initially carried by the victim-ego and the alienated ego. The hidden, traumatized "true self" is returned to life, as is the burden carrier, through experiences that feel like grace, and through finding access to the parental archetypes in the ritual caldron of analysis. Then the parts can heal and develop. But both parts return to life with their extraordinary visions of sacrifice, separation, grief, confusion, sheer emptiness and evil. They have intimate knowledge of shadow and suffering. Such vision must be integrated into a new concept of reality or the godhead. Only when one's experiences can be seen as meaningfully related to an image of the transpersonal, can the scapegoat-identified individual find the self-acceptance necessary for life. Many such persons come to recognize that the dark side of the godhead is a palpable force—one that merits the respect of conscious confrontation. Within the context of the amoral "phenomenon" of the divinity,[88] the human shadow finds its transpersonal meaning and purpose. It participates in the paradox of divine order and disorder.

Such perception is hard won. It is what the patriarchs of religions shield humankind from knowing when they circumscribe reality and the godhead with the ideals of virtue. Paradoxically, it is also those very virtues, and their companion vices, which create scapegoating and through it the potential development of the consciousness and conscience capable of relating to the reality behind what is called virtue and vice. And the shields themselves are valuable, for only the strong, disciplined and devoted can bear to penetrate to such paradoxical and painful awareness of the multivalent wholeness of life. Those who suffer the scapegoat complex are among those called to such a view, which is acquired both through, and in order to find, the healing of the complex.

Notes

Refer to Bibliography for publication details not given here.

1. Mary Douglas, *Purity and Danger: An Analysis of Concepts of Pollution and Taboo*, p. 53.
2. Jerome Kagan, "The Parental Love Trap," *Psychology Today* (August 1978), p. 54.
3. Matthew 5:48, King James Version.
4. Jung, *Mysterium Coniunctionis*, CW 14, par. 117.
5. See especially James G. Frazer, *The Scapegoat;* R. DeVerteuil, "The Scapegoat Archetype"; Hyam Maccoby, *The Sacred Executioner: Human Sacrifice and the Legend of Guilt;* John B. Vickery and J'nan M. Sellery, eds., *The Scapegoat: Ritual and Literature.*
6. See Gertrude Ujhely, "Thoughts Concerning the *Causa Finalis* of the Cognitive Mode Inherent in Pre-Oedipal Psychopathology," and Edward C. Whitmont, "The Magic Dimensions of the Unconscious."
7. Theodor H. Gaster, *Festivals of the Jewish Year,* pp. 138-139.
8. See Jung, "A Psychological View of Conscience," *Civilization in Transition,* CW 10.
9. Ibid., par. 852.
10. Ibid., par. 855. See also "The Transcendent Function," *The Structure and Dynamics of the Psyche,* CW 8.
11. *Participation mystique* is a term derived from the anthropologist Lucien Lévy-Bruhl. Jung writes: "It denotes a peculiar kind of psychological connection . . . [in which] the subject cannot clearly distinguish himself from the object but is bound to it by a direct relationship which amounts to partial *identity.*" ("Definitions," *Psychological Types,* CW 6, par. 781)
12. There is a modulated survival of such fertility orgies on Yom Kippur reported in the Mishna. In it young girls from Jerusalem danced in the vineyards dressed in white finery to attract suitors. See Gaster, *Festivals of the Jewish Year,* pp. 148-149.
13. E. Neumann, *The Child,* p. 128.
14. Douglas, p. 48.
15. Ibid., p. 53.
16. In Wole Soyinka's Nigerian drama about a scapegoat, the schoolmaster is stoned and exiled, taking the place of the original scapegoat, a poor tramp. The schoolmaster was the offender because he was unusually educated, sensitive and empathic.
17. Frazer, *The New Golden Bough,* pars. 439-466.

111

18. Dionysus of Halicarnassus, quoted by Jessie Weston, *From Ritual to Romance,* p. 92. Frazer identifies Mamurius Veturius as "the old Mars," the old year's vegetation divinity who was beaten on his genitals to purify and enhance procreative potential, then slain to make space for the new year's reborn and vigorous fertility god.

19. Frazer, *New Golden Bough,* par. 462.

20. See Jean Baker Miller, *Toward a New Psychology of Women.*

21. Jung, "A Psychological View of Conscience," CW 10, par. 830.

22. See Jung, *Psychological Types,* CW 6, pars. 638-643 (introverted feeling), and 655-663 (introverted intuition).

23. A family may of course contain more than one child who is identified with the scapegoat, with each carrying different aspects of the parental and collective shadows.

24. Neumann, *The Child,* p. 86.

25. In scapegoat-identified individuals there is generally a faint image of having once been accepted. They tend to feel there was one peripheral person who valued their being. This sustains the hidden ego—or "true self" in D.W. Winnicott's term (see *The Maturational Processes and the Facilitating Environment*)—and staves off the total fear and self-hate that can lead to psychosis.

26. R.D. Laing, *The Divided Self: An Existential Study of Sanity and Madness* (Pelican Books, London, 1965), pp. 42-43.

27. Leviticus 16:16, Jerusalem Bible.

28. Louis Ginzberg, *The Legends of the Jews,* vol. 1, p. 148.

29. Leviticus 16:21, Jerusalem Bible.

30. Ibid., 16:22.

31. Rivkah Kluger, *Satan in the Old Testament,* p. 48.

32. William Butler Yeats, *The Collected Poems* (Macmillan Company, New York, 1956), p. 184.

33. Ginzberg, vol. 1, p. 125.

34. Maccoby states that the etymology of *Azazel* derives from *ez,* "the goat," and *azal,* "to go" or "to escape" (p. 189). Rabbinic authority derives the name from "hard mountain" or "rock."

35. Kluger, p. 48.

36. Maccoby argues that Azazel "may be a name originally given to the Sacred Executioner himself" (p. 189), that priestly perpetrator of the human sacrifice which appeased an angry God. The Sacred Executioner then bore the gratitude and guilt of the community. He was banished into the wilderness to roam freely after his essential, atoning action. There he bore the distinguishing mark of the red thread used to sprinkle the sacrificed victim's blood. He was a feared

outlaw, but one identified with the desert god and so under divine protection. He thus suffered "privileged banishment" (pp. 22, 34-36).

37. DeVerteuil, p. 212.
38. Ginzberg, vol. 5, p. 171.
39. Gershom Scholem, *Major Trends in Jewish Mysticism,* p. 237.
40. See Marie-Louise von Franz, *Shadow and Evil in Fairytales,* p. 147.
41. Douglas, p. 117.
42. For example, Inanna's descent to *kur,* the realm of Ereshkigal and the collective shadow; Christ's encounter with the temptations of the archetypal power drive in the form of Satan; and Buddha's withdrawal to achieve Enlightenment.
43. See, for example, Salvador Minuchin, *Families and Family Therapy* (Harvard University Press, Cambridge, 1974).
44. Douglas, p. 51.
45. Jung, "A Psychological View of Conscience," CW 10, pars. 849-852.
46. Edward C. Whitmont, *Return of the Goddess,* pp. 40ff.
47. Karen Horney, *Neurosis and Human Growth: The Struggle toward Self-Realization* (W.W. Norton, New York, 1950), pp. 64-65.
48. Otto Kernberg, *Borderline Conditions and Pathological Narcissism,* p. 30.
49. Marion Woodman, *Addiction to Perfection: The Still Unravished Bride.*
50. This is one of the hazards when the analyst has not worked through his or her own scapegoat complex. A power problem can easily develop, distorting the analyst's access to shadow material and inhibiting empathic openness to the depths of raw emotionality.
51. See Frazer, *The Scapegoat.*
52. See Maccoby, *The Sacred Executioner,* and Jacques Soustelle, *Daily Life of the Aztecs.*
53. Hans Kohut writes: "In order to escape from depression, the child turns from the unempathic or absent self-object to oral, anal, and phallic sensations which he experiences with great intensity. . . . [Such] act[s] gave . . . fleetingly a feeling of strength and heightened self-esteem [but they were] of course, unable to fill the structural defect from which he suffered, and thus had to be repeated again and again—the patient was indeed addicted to it" (*The Restoration of the Self,* p. 122). Powerfully experienced affect states themselves have a similar effect, and scapegoat-identified individuals can likewise be addicted to rage, despair, longing or sex as readily as to foods, alcohol or drugs.

54. Since the complex is so widespread, such adversarial attacks are an omnipresent collective danger.

55. Gaster, *Myth, Legend and Custom in the Old Testament,* p. 581.

56. On the level of societal groups, such behavior operates all too often as the basis of "justifiable" wars.

57. Just before this woman came into therapy, she had been deprived of the main current focus of her vengeance because her husband had left her. Then the assertive libido regressed to a more passive form and turned against her own victim-ego. She became doom-ridden and suicidal. The vengeance expressed in the dream indicated a return of assertive capacities up the spectrum toward supporting her own survival. This mode of aggression can be worked with more easily in therapy to affirm and tame the instinctive energy.

58. See Jung, *The Visions Seminars,* pp. 212-213.

59. See Sylvia Brinton Perera, "Ceremonies of the Emerging Ego in Psychotherapy."

60. Jung, *Psychology and Alchemy,* CW 12, par. 152.

61. See Perera, "Ceremonies of the Emerging Ego in Psychotherapy."

62. The model of analytic work based only upon frustration of needs can inhibit any healing in schizoid, scapegoat-identified individuals. The danger is that the therapist may be cast in the role of depriving accuser, or helpless victim of the imperatives of "analysis," while the patient unconsciously colludes with the therapist, endlessly playing out the complex.

63. See Edward F. Edinger, *Anatomy of the Psyche,* chapter 4.

64. On such a level of interaction the concept of projection does not seem to apply. The fusion of the scapegoat with the community is magical and symbiotic. Healing of the other merges into healing of the scapegoated one who is fused with the other, for the caretaker keeps his or her reality alive by sensing its location in others and nurturing it there. This is closely analogous to the primitive embeddedness of the pre-individual in the tribe, and the child in the mother-child symbiotic field, which are both forms of *participation mystique* (see above, note 11).

65. Frazer, *New Golden Bough,* par. 462.

66. Ibid.

67. See Perera, *Descent to the Goddess: A Way of Initiation for Women.*

68. It is invaluable to have some reference to a beneficent figure from childhood on which to anchor current learning. When the only such memories are of childhood peers, the work must go slowly enough to "grow them up." When there are no remembered, constantly-caring figures, the wounds of self-hate open easily under stress and require

constant attention. In such situations the transference itself may need to open to the near-psychotic levels where the victim-ego has hidden, but this is not always possible.

69. Edward F. Edinger, personal communication.

70. Enki or Ea was a water and wisdom creator god sometimes depicted as a goat with a fish tail, the original deity of the constellation Capricorn. It was he who released the goddess Inanna, the first scapegoat in literature, from underworld exile in *kur*, the wilderness. (See Perera, *Descent to the Goddess*)

71. Pan, the hairy, goat-footed one, Horned God of the Witches (see Margaret Murray, *The God of the Witches*), and Satan are thus in the lineage of Azazel.

72. This same name, Ninamaskug, was given to Dumuzi, the annually dying and restored shepherd god and Year King consort of the goddess Inanna. (See Perera, *Descent to the Goddess*)

73. Stephen H. Langdon, *Mythology of All Races*, vol. 5, *Semitic*, p. 356.

74. For material on this motif in another part of the Western world, see Anne Ross, *Pagan Celtic Britain* (Columbia University Press, New York, 1967).

75. See Ralph Whitlock, *In Search of Lost Gods: A Guide to British Folklore*, p. 177.

76. Edward C. Whitmont, personal communication.

77. See Edward F. Edinger, "The Tragic Hero: An Image of Individuation," p. 68.

78. Jung, "A Psychological View of Conscience," CW 10, par. 856.

79. Jung, "The Fight with the Shadow," CW 10, par. 456.

80. Erich Neumann, *Depth Psychology and a New Ethic*, p. 130.

81. Judges 5:24, Jerusalem Bible.

82. Neumann, *Depth Psychology*, p. 103.

83. See Edward F. Edinger, *The Creation of Consciousness: Jung's Myth for Modern Man*, p. 11.

84. Idris Shad, *Tales of the Dervishes*, pp. 63-65.

85. Even groups which start as task-oriented fall into the more primitive form when their cooperative focus becomes blurred or so complex that factions form around its implementation, or when they become so large that members cannot share with each other in order to find areas of undefensive mutuality and respect.

86. See Edward C. Whitmont, *Return of the Goddess*, pp. 255-256, and "Individual Transformation and Personal Responsibility," *Quadrant*, vol. 19, no. 1 (Spring 1986). He suggests the necessity of new forms of group self-confrontation through the mutual "leveling" of indi-

vidual members. The literature on group and family dynamics supports both the efficacy of such forms and the potential for learning new modes of consciousness through group and family therapy.

87. See Edward F. Edinger, "Christ as Paradigm of the Individuating Ego," in *Ego and Archetype: Individuation and the Religious Function of the Psyche.*

88. See Jung, "Answer to Job," *Psychology West and East,* CW 11, par. 600. Yahweh's behavior toward Job, writes Jung, is that of "an unconscious being who cannot be judged morally. Yahweh is a *phenomenon* and, as Job says, 'not a man.' "

Glossary of Jungian Terms

Anima (Latin, "soul"). The unconscious, feminine side of a man's personality. She is personified in dreams by images of women ranging from prostitute and seductress to spiritual guide (Wisdom). She is the eros principle, hence a man's anima development is reflected in how he relates to women. Identification with the anima can appear as moodiness, effeminacy, and oversensitivity. Jung calls the anima *the archetype of life itself.*

Animus (Latin, "spirit"). The unconscious, masculine side of a woman's personality. He personifies the logos principle. Identification with the animus can cause a woman to become rigid, opinionated, and argumentative. More positively, he is the inner man who acts as a bridge between the woman's ego and her own creative resources in the unconscious.

Archetypes. Irrepresentable in themselves, but their effects appear in consciousness as the archetypal images and ideas. These are universal patterns or motifs which come from the collective unconscious and are the basic content of religions, mythologies, legends, and fairytales. They emerge in individuals through dreams and visions.

Association. A spontaneous flow of interconnected thoughts and images around a specific idea, determined by unconscious connections.

Complex. An emotionally charged group of ideas or images. At the "center" of a complex is an archetype or archetypal image.

Constellate. Whenever there is a strong emotional reaction to a person or a situation, a complex has been constellated (activated).

Ego. The central complex in the field of consciousness. A strong ego can relate objectively to activated contents of the unconscious (i.e., other complexes), rather than identifying with them, which appears as a state of possession.

Feeling. One of the four psychic functions. It is a rational function which evaluates the worth of relationships and situations. Feeling must be distinguished from emotion, which is due to an activated complex.

Individuation. The conscious realization of one's unique psychological reality, including both strengths and limitations. It leads to the experience of the Self as the regulating center of the psyche.

Inflation. A state in which one has an unrealistically high or low (negative inflation) sense of identity. It indicates a regression of consciousness into unconsciousness, which typically happens when the ego takes too many unconscious contents upon itself and loses the faculty of discrimination.

Intuition. One of the four psychic functions. It is the irrational function which tells us the possibilities inherent in the present. In contrast to sensation (the function which perceives immediate reality through the physical senses) intuition perceives via the unconscious, e.g., flashes of insight of unknown origin.

117

Participation mystique. A term derived from the anthropologist Lévy-Bruhl, denoting a primitive, psychological connection with objects, or between persons, resulting in a strong unconscious bond.

Persona (Latin, "actor's mask"). One's social role, derived from the expectations of society and early training. A strong ego relates to the outside world through a flexible persona; identification with a specific persona (doctor, scholar, artist, etc.) inhibits psychological development.

Projection. The process whereby an unconscious quality or characteristic of one's own is perceived and reacted to in an outer object or person. Projection of the anima or animus onto a real women or man is experienced as falling in love. Frustrated expectations indicate the need to withdraw projections, in order to relate to the reality of other people.

Puer aeternus (Latin, "eternal youth"). Indicates a certain type of man who remains too long in adolescent psychology, generally associated with a strong unconscious attachment to the mother (actual or symbolic). Positive traits are spontaneity and openness to change. His female counterpart is the **puella,** an "eternal girl" with a corresponding attachment to the father-world.

Self. The archetype of wholeness and the regulating center of the personality. It is experienced as a transpersonal power which transcends the ego, e.g., God.

Senex (Latin, "old man"). Associated with attitudes that come with advancing age. Negatively, this can mean cynicism, rigidity and extreme conservatism; positive traits are responsibility, orderliness and self-discipline. A well-balanced personality functions appropriately within the puer-senex polarity.

Shadow. An unconscious part of the personality characterized by traits and attitudes, whether negative or positive, which the conscious ego tends to reject or ignore. It is personified in dreams by persons of the same sex as the dreamer. Consciously assimilating one's shadow usually results in an increase of energy.

Symbol. The best possible expression for something essentially unknown. Symbolic thinking is non-linear, right-brain oriented; it is complementary to logical, linear, left-brain thinking.

Transcendent function. The reconciling "third" which emerges from the unconscious (in the form of a symbol or a new attitude) after the conflicting opposites have been consciously differentiated, and the tension between them held.

Transference and countertransference. Particular cases of projection, commonly used to describe the unconscious, emotional bonds that arise between two persons in an analytic or therapeutic relationship.

Uroboros. The mythical snake or dragon that eats its own tail. It is a symbol both for individuation as a self-contained, circular process, and for narcissistic self-absorption.

Select Bibliography

DeVerteuil, R. "The Scapegoat Archetype." *Journal of Religion and Health,* vol. 5, no. 3 (1966).

Douglas, Mary. *Purity and Danger: An Analysis of Concepts of Pollution and Taboo.* Routledge & Kegan Paul, London, 1966.

Edinger, Edward F. *Anatomy of the Psyche.* Open Court, La Salle, IL, 1985.

——. *The Creation of Consciousness: Jung's Myth for Modern Man.* Inner City Books, Toronto, 1984.

——. *Ego and Archetype: Individuation and the Religious Function of the Psyche.* G.P. Putnam's Sons, New York, 1972.

——. "The Tragic Hero: An Image of Individuation." *Parabola,* vol. 1, no. 1 (1976).

Fordham, Michael. *Jungian Psychotherapy: A Study in Analytical Psychology.* John Wiley & Sons, New York, 1978.

Frazer, James George. *The New Golden Bough.* Ed. Theodor H. Gaster. Anchor Books, New York, 1961.

——. *The Scapegoat,* vol. 9 of *The Golden Bough: A Study in Magic and Religion.* Macmillan & Co., London, 1920.

Gaster, Theodor H. *Festivals of the Jewish New Year.* William Sloane, New York, 1952.

——. *Myth, Legend and Custom in the Old Testament.* Harper & Row, New York, 1969.

Ginzberg, Louis. *The Legends of the Jews.* Jewish Publication Society of America, Philadelphia, 1909.

Guntrip, Harry. *Schizoid Phenomena, Object Relations and the Self.* International Universities Press, New York, 1969.

Harrison, Jane. *Prolegomena to the Study of Greek Religion.* Cambridge University Press, Cambridge, 1922.

The Jerusalem Bible. Doubleday & Co., Garden City, NY, 1966.

Jung, C.G. *The Collected Works* (Bollingen Series XX). 20 vols. Trans. R.F.C. Hull. Ed. H. Read, M. Fordham, G. Adler, Wm. McGuire. Princeton University Press, Princeton, 1953-1979.

——. *The Visions Seminars* (1930-1934). Spring Publications, Zurich, 1976.

Kahn, M. Masud R. *The Privacy of the Self: Papers on Psychoanalytic Theory and Technique.* International Universities Press, New York, 1974.

——. *Hidden Selves: Between Theory and Practice in Psychoanalysis.* International Universities Press, New York, 1983.

119

Kernberg, Otto. *Borderline Conditions and Pathological Narcissism*. Jason Aronson, New York, 1975.

Kluger, Rivkah. *Satan in the Old Testament*. Northwestern University Press, Evanston, IL, 1967.

Kohut, Heinz. *The Restoration of the Self*. International Universities Press, New York, 1977.

Langdon, Stephen H. *Mythology of All Races,* vol. 5: *Semitic*. Archaeological Institute of America, Boston, 1931.

Maccoby, Hyam. *The Sacred Executioner: Human Sacrifice and the Legend of Guilt*. Thames & Hudson, London, 1982.

Meltzer, Donald. *The Clinical Significance of the Work of Bion*. Clunie Press, Perthshire, 1978.

Miller, Jean Baker. *Toward a New Psychology of Women*. Beacon Press, Boston, 1976.

Murray, Margaret. *The God of the Witches*. Oxford University Press, London, 1931.

Neumann, Eric. *The Child*. G.P. Putnam's Sons, New York, 1973.

―――. *Depth Psychology and a New Ethic*. G.P. Putnam's Sons, New York, 1969.

Ogden, Thomas H. *Projective Identification and Psychotherapeutic Technique*. Jason Aronson, New York, 1982.

Perera, Sylvia Brinton. "Ceremonies of the Emerging Ego in Psychotherapy." *Chiron: A Review of Jungian Analysis,* 1986.

―――. *Descent to the Goddess: A Way of Initiation for Women*. Inner City Books, Toronto, 1981.

Perry, John Weir. *Roots of Renewal in Myth and Madness*. Jossey-Boss, San Francisco, 1976.

Roscher, W.H. and Hillman, James. *Pan and the Nightmare: Two Essays*. Spring Publications, New York, 1972.

Scholem, Gershom. *Major Trends in Jewish Mysticism*. Schocken Books, New York, 1941.

Schwartz-Salant, Nathan. *Narcissism and Character Transformation: The Psychology of Narcissistic Character Disorders*. Inner City Books, Toronto, 1982.

Searles, H.F. *Countertransference*. University Press, New York, 1979.

Shah, Idris. *Tales of the Dervishes*. Dutton, New York, 1969.

Soustelle, Jacques. *Daily Life of the Aztecs*. London, 1961.

Ujhely, Gertrude. "Thoughts Concerning the *Causa Finalis* of the Cognitive Mode Inherent in Pre-Oedipal Psychopathology." Diploma Thesis, C.G. Jung Institute of New York, 1980.

Vickery, John B. and Sellery, J'nan M., eds. *The Scapegoat: Ritual and Literature*. Houghton Mifflin, Boston, 1972.

Von Franz, Marie-Louise. *Shadow and Evil in Fairy Tales*. Spring Publications, Zurich, 1974.

Weston, Jessie. *From Ritual to Romance*. Doubleday Anchor Books, New York, 1957.

Whitlock, Ralph. *In Search of Lost Gods: A Guide to British Folklore*. Phaidon Press, Oxford, 1979.

Whitmont, Edward C. "Individual Transformation and Personal Responsibility." *Quadrant*, vol. 18, no. 2 (1985).

————. "The Magic Dimension of the Unconscious," in *Dynamic Aspects of the Psyche*. Analytical Psychology Club of New York, New York, n.d.

————. *Return of the Goddess*. Crossroad, New York, 1982.

Winnicott, D.W. *The Maturational Processes and the Facilitating Environment*. International Universities Press, New York, 1965.

————. *Playing and Reality*. Basic Books, New York, 1971.

Woodman, Marion. *Addiction to Perfection: The Still Unravished Bride*. Inner City Books, Toronto, 1982.

————. *The Pregnant Virgin: A Process of Psychological Transformation*. Inner City Books, Toronto, 1985.

Index

6. Descent to the Goddess: A Way of Initiation for Women.
Sylvia Brinton Perera (New York). ISBN 0-919123-05-8. 112 pp. $12

A highly original and provocative book about women's freedom and the need for an inner, female authority in a masculine-oriented society.

Combining ancient texts and modern dreams, the author, a practising Jungian analyst, presents a way of feminine initiation. Inanna-Ishtar, Sumerian Goddess of Heaven and Earth, journeys into the underworld to Ereshkigal, her dark "sister," and returns. So modern women must descend from their old role-determined behavior into the depths of their instinct and image patterns, to find anew the Great Goddess and restore her values to modern culture.

Men too will be interested in this book, both for its revelations of women's essential nature and for its implications in terms of their own inner journey.

"The most significant contribution to an understanding of feminine psychology since Esther Harding's *The Way of All Women.*"—**Marion Woodman,** Jungian analyst and author of *Addiction to Perfection, The Pregnant Virgin* and *The Owl Was a Baker's Daughter.*

Marie-Louise von Franz, Honorary Patron

Studies in Jungian Psychology
by Jungian Analysts
Limited Edition Paperbacks

EDWARD F. EDINGER, M.D. (Los Angeles)
The Creation of Consciousness: Jung's Myth for Modern Man. $13
Explores the significance of Jung's life and work, in terms of the meaning of human life. Illus.
Encounter with the Self: William Blake's *Illustrations of the Book of Job.* $10
A penetrating commentary on the Job story. Illustrated with Blake's original 22 engravings.
The Bible and the Psyche: Individuation Symbolism in the Old Testament. $15
A major new work relating biblical events to the individual movement toward wholeness.

MARION WOODMAN (Toronto)
Addiction to Perfection: The Still Unravished Bride. $15
A powerful and authoritative look at the psychology and attitudes of modern women. Illustrated.
The Pregnant Virgin: A Process of Psychological Transformation. $16
A celebration of the feminine, in both men and women, and the search for personal identity. Ill.
The Owl Was a Baker's Daughter: Obesity and Anorexia Nervosa. $14
Focus on the body as mirror of the psyche in eating disorders and weight problems. Illustrated.

MARIE-LOUISE VON FRANZ (Zurich)
The Psychological Meaning of Redemption Motifs in Fairytales. $13
Unique account of the significance of fairytales for an understanding of the individuation process.
On Divination and Synchronicity: Psychology of Meaningful Chance. $13
Penetrating study of the meaning of the irrational and methods of divining fate (such as I Ching).
Alchemy: An Introduction to the Symbolism and the Psychology. $18
Invaluable for interpreting images and motifs in modern dreams and drawings. 84 Illustrations.

SYLVIA BRINTON PERERA (New York)
Descent to the Goddess. A Way of Initiation for Women. $12
A provocative study of the need for an inner, female authority in a masculine-oriented society.
The Scapegoat Complex: Toward a Mythology of Shadow and Guilt. $13
A hard-hitting exploration of scapegoat psychology as it manifests in modern men and women.

JAMES A. HALL, M.D. (Dallas)
Jungian Dream Interpretation: A Handbook of Theory and Practice. $13
A practical guide, with many clinical examples. Particular attention to common dream motifs.
The Jungian Experience: Analysis and Individuation. $15
A comprehensive presentation of the clinical application of Jung's model of the psyche.

ALDO CAROTENUTO (Rome)
The Vertical Labyrinth: Individuation in Jungian Psychology. $14
A guided journey through the world of dreams and psychic reality. Rich in analytical insights.
The Spiral Way: A Woman's Healing Journey. $14
The case history of a 50-year-old woman's Jungian analysis. Emphasis on dream interpretation.

Prices and payment in $US (except for Canadian orders).
Please add $1 per book (bookpost) or $3 per book (airmail).
Send check or money order (no Credit Cards).

Write for complete Catalogue

INNER CITY BOOKS
Box 1271, Station Q, Toronto, Canada M4T 2P4   (416) 927-0355